TURNING MONEY INTO REBELLION

The Unlikely Story of Denmark's Revolutionary Bank Robbers

edited and translated by Gabriel Kuhn

PMPRESS

KER
SPL
EBE
DEB

2014

Turning Money into Rebellion:
The Unlikely Story of Denmark's Revolutionary Bank Robbers

Edited and translated by Gabriel Kuhn

copyright PM Press, 2014

ISBN: 9781604863161
Library of Congress Control Number: 2013956927

Kersplebedeb Publishing and Distribution
CP 63560
CCCP Van Horne
Montreal, Quebec
Canada H3W 3H8
www.kersplebedeb.com
www.leftwingbooks.net

PM Press
P.O. Box 23912
Oakland, CA 94623
www.pmpress.org

Layout by Kersplebedeb
Cover Design by John Yates

Printed in the USA by the Employee Owners of
Thomson-Shore in Dexter, Michigan
www.thomsonshore.com

Contents

About the Authors

Gabriel Kuhn is an Austrian-born author and translator living in Stockholm, Sweden. He has been involved in internationalist projects for twenty-five years. Among his publications with PM Press are Life Under the Jolly Roger: Reflections on Golden Age Piracy *(2010),* Sober Living for the Revolution: Hardcore Punk, Straight Edge, and Radical Politics *(2010), and* Soccer vs. the State: Tackling Football and Radical Politics *(2011).*

Klaus Viehmann was a member of the 2nd of June Movement, a German urban guerrilla group. He was arrested in 1978 and spent fifteen years in prison. Today, he lives as a typesetter and graphic designer in Berlin. PM Press and Kersplebedeb have published his pamphlet Prison Round Trip *(2009).*

Craftsmen of World Revolution

The essence of the Blekingegade Group was international solidarity.[1] A solidarity that "you can hold in your hands." Concretely, money. Lots of money. Acquired in robberies in the metropolitan North and passed on to the tricontinental South.[2] For many years. Respect!

Many have had the idea of taking money from the rich, revolutionaries among them. Indeed: amid palatial banks and abundant wealth it is easy to wonder why analyses of capitalism fill miles' worth of bookshelves while big money is still flowing from the bottom to the top. Besides, an action to acquire money might be less humiliating than sending out yet another grant application. And wouldn't it feel good to relieve a project in Latin America or a group in Southeast Asia from the eternal hunt for funds? Wasn't there a man in Catalonia who took a big loan and passed the money on to political militants? Wasn't there an anarchist who channeled millions to the movement by mastering the art of forging checks?

---

1. To keep things simple, the name "Blekingegade Group" will be used in this preface as a rough synonym both for the political organizations KAK and M-KA and for the illegal structures they contained. The book will provide a detailed history of these organizations and structures and of their internal dynamics. —K.V.

2. In 1966, the Tricontinental Conference in Havana, Cuba, brought together representatives of political organizations from Africa, Asia, and Latin America. Following the conference, the radical and anti-imperialist left in Germany adopted the abbreviation "Trikont" as a common signifier for the three continents. Despite there being no similar abbreviation commonly used in English, the term has been translated as "tricont" in this preface, since the closest alternative, "Third World" (Dritte Welt in German, on occasion also used in the preface and translated accordingly), has both different origins and connotations. The opposite of the "tricont" is the "metropole," that is, the industrialized nations in the global North. —Ed.

Unfortunately, among the side effects of "expropriation forte" are repression and prison sentences. A sustainable redistribution of funds needs solid craftsmanship if it wants to rest on golden floors. People engaging in such activities must have answers to a few questions: What do you want from life? Self-realization? Personal happiness? The happiness of others? Who are these others? How far away are they? Does solidarity end with your family, your friends, your country, or your continent? Is your aspiration to make a revolutionary commitment or to temporarily join a working group? Do you want to grow old with your political practice? The existential framework required for illegal practice is not always comfortable: organizational discipline instead of personal self-realization, continuity instead of spontaneity, a bourgeois facade instead of subcultural havens, solid convictions instead of discursive formations, secrecy instead of openness, selflessness instead of identity politics, and so on.

The individual motivation—perhaps also the precondition—for the craft of acquiring money is the hope that you are able to contribute to a new world, to effectively harm the powerful, to overcome capitalist alienation, to create meaningful ways of living instead of "being lived." This might sound terribly existentialist, but social being and political consciousness—in other words, thinking and acting—have never been one-way streets. To sever the dialectical relationship between practical experience and analytical reflection leads to a dead end, the consequence being either academic inaction or spontaneous actionism, neither of which provides a solid ground for organized solidarity. Inaction produces nothing that "can be held in your hands," and spontaneous actionism might be beautiful, but the struggle for liberation is long and not always exciting. The history of many movements suggests that each political generation only has the strength to rebel once, even if this strength lasts a long time in some individuals, probably because they are socially organized in a way that allows for extended collective reflection.

In an abstract sense, (international) solidarity means to establish a relationship between political subjects, people, and organizations. It is not based on projecting your visions of revolution onto objects of charity. In a proper relationship of solidarity, no one is stuck in awe worshiping "leaders," and no one allows others to make decisions for them. Discussions happen on a level playing field, and people give according to necessity and conviction without cutting deals. It is a relationship based on basic human interaction, not on formalities. Solidarity, in this sense, doesn't mean searching for a new struggle every few years when you have become disillusioned with the last one; it doesn't mean looking for the next best place "where things are happening," or for new "heroes," as soon as the former ones are gone or have proven themselves corrupted.

The Blekingegade Group was a child of the late 1960s. Its members were Marxists-Leninists, even if of a special kind. The persistency with which they supported "national liberation movements" and refugee camps for almost twenty years distinguished their practice from the kind of solidarity whizzing across the globe: Vietnam, Palestine, South Africa, Zimbabwe, Chile, Portugal, Spain, Nicaragua ... The group's members were more determined than the proletarian impersonators of the 1970s who soon retreated to the "alternative middle class."

As far as we know, no other Marxist-Leninist group has maintained a clandestine infrastructure for illegal actions and the acquisition of money for so long. And no other has propagated the so-called "parasite state theory," which, essentially, brought together two theses: first, the ("Maoist") one expressed in Che Guevara's speech at the Tricontinental Conference, with the "Third World" being the engine of world revolution and "villages encircling cities." This view became particularly popular following the period of decolonization and the defeat of the USA in Vietnam. The second thesis contended that the working class in the metropole had been "muted" and pacified by the imperialist bourgeoisie, which handed to the metropolitan workers a portion of the superprofits from the exploitation of human and natural resources in the tricont. This resulted in a "labor aristocracy" (Lenin) that had already rallied around the concept of the "nation" during World War I and showed the same reaction in the global context of the 1970s. "Social Partnership" was more important than solidarity with working-class peers in the tricont.

The Blekingegade Group's strategy derived from combining these two assumptions. Any attempt by a revolutionary minority to mobilize the "masses" in the metropole was considered futile as long as the superprofits were flowing in. Hence, the flow needed to be stopped, which required strengthening movements in the tricont and enabling them to win. This is the reason for the Blekingegade Group turning its attention to such movements in the early 1970s, particularly in the Middle East and in Southern Africa, and for supplying them with money and material for years. (The fact that the Palestinian PFLP became the group's most important partner was likely due to the PFLP's presence in Western Europe and its aggressive socialist/internationalist orientation.)

The Blekingegade Group always reflected on the political-economic conditions for their anti-imperialist money transfers, at times adopting notions that were uncharacteristic for Marxist-Leninist groups. For example, they felt that the relationship between the metropole and the tricont was defined by "unequal exchange," and advocated the "delinking" of decolonized countries from the global market. Surprisingly, there was less reflection on crucial questions of revolutionary strategy, or at least this is how it appears in retrospect. For example, one of the conclusions drawn by members doing factory work in Frankfurt in 1974 was that workers in Western Europe weren't interested in left-wing leaflets; this was taken as yet another reason for prioritizing the support of liberation movements. Fine. However, had the Blekingegade Group brought left-wing leaflets instead of money to Beirut or South Africa, would anyone there have been interested in them? Or, to put it the other way around: how would the group have been received in Germany had it provided money to the migrant laborers fighting both German skilled workers and bosses?

Regarding the "parasite state theory," this is what we can state today: *one* determinant—the economic interest—cannot sufficiently explain the relative peace in the metropole. Is the (male) working class not also "muted" by the patriarchal exploitation of women? Are "white" workers not "muted" by the racist exploitation of migrant labor? Are techniques of domination, such as "cultural hegemony" (Gramsci), not too diverse to be determined by the economy alone? Is alienation (the psychological situation) not related to the material reality of the working class? Can people, considering all of the fears and the deception they are facing, even name their "objective interests"? Would they really sacrifice peace, health, and happiness for a second car? To make things even more complicated, most of these questions also apply to the conditions in the tricont; the old dichotomy of "metropole" vs. "Third World" was never more than a partial truth.

The socialist world revolution whose necessity the Blekingegade Group members were convinced of—as are many leftists today, even if they no longer dare say it—is only an imagined and idealized turning point, no concrete guidepost. A messianic project can never provide direction for—possibly illegal—everyday political action. Even if the global market determines our everyday life in many ways, concrete decisions cannot be derived from abstract laws; the contradictory conditions and multifaceted desires of people in their specific environments need to be understood and acknowledged. No one can escape the complex global web of imperialism/colonialism, nationalism, capitalism, patriarchy, and racism; there are no simple and eternal truths, nor is there one main contradiction.

Capitalism and the global market have developed enormously since the 1980s. The class struggle from above (some even speak of "refeudalization") and the backlash against all forms of rebellion not exploitable by Google or Apple clearly have the upper hand. The metropolitan working class remains quiet; or it is kept quiet by means of hegemony and repression, particularly in places where "muting" it in a traditional Fordist manner ended after the collapse of the Soviet Union. We can see some sparks at the precarious margins, but there is no prairie fire. Superprofits keep on flowing from old and new sources, military capacities are increasingly asymmetrical, and the "villages" are full of contradictions. Some of them, such as China, have become "cities," while the crisis threatens to turn some of the "cities" on Europe's periphery into "villages." "National liberation movements" such as the Nicaraguan FSLN, the PFLP, or the South African ANC have lost their emancipatory potential under the pressure of the balances of power and due to their own mistakes. Cuba and guerrilla groups such as the Colombian FARC and ELN still exist—not without flaws and with no prospect of victory, but they are here, which must count as a success in light of all the movements that have been destroyed or co-opted during the last thirty to forty years. There have been Pyrrhic victories against authoritarian rule such as the end of the apartheid regime and the "Arab Spring"; there have been emancipatory developments in countries like Venezuela and Bolivia; there have been new strike waves and new forms of organizing in India, China, and Bangladesh. For anti-racist groups, collaboration with transnational migrants and refugees has become commonplace. Visits to the Lacandon jungle are much easier today than travels to African refugee camps were in the 1970s. Current international meetings of social movements seem to be much less hierarchical than former "cadre contacts with foreign comrades." Days of action such as Blockupy and anti-summit mobilizations from Seattle to Genoa to Heiligendamm mark transnational campaigns that were not possible thirty years ago.

So far, so good? Are the questions raised above, questions of individual commitment and definitions of solidarity, now answered? Are we still trying to "overthrow all relations in which man is a debased, enslaved, abandoned, despicable essence"? Do we live or "are we lived"? Is revolutionary transformation in the metropole a precondition for global justice? What does a contemporary revolutionary strategy look like? Is the notion of (world) revolution outdated? Perhaps people simply no longer ask these questions after they have so often been, quietly and shamefully, removed from the agenda of a left defeated by hostile social conditions and overwhelming repression? Perhaps the urgency of these questions has been psychologically repressed? But psychological repression is no substitute for political discussion, especially when it is impossible for the metropolitan left to escape questions that inevitably surface in other countries and under different historical circumstances.

The Blekingegade Group was no urban guerrilla. Its revolutionary subject was located in the tricont, not in the neighborhood or the factory. The group did not attack the state, it issued no communiqués, and it disguised its robberies as criminal actions. It never had to justify its political practice to the left or to the wider public. It wasn't looking for, and didn't need, a broad base. Going public would have only meant danger; it had no propagandistic value. The group's members never went completely underground, and for a long time there were no prisoners. All of this differentiated the Blekingegade Group from urban guerrillas active in West Germany or Italy. The Blekingegade Group consciously avoided contact with the Red Army

Faction, the Second of June Movement, and the Red Brigades in order not to become a target of "anti-terrorist" repression. Some parallels can be drawn to the Revolutionary Cells in Germany. Members of the Revolutionary Cells also lived relatively secure lives aboveground, engaging in an action every year or two. We can only speculate if the Blekingegade Group would have ended in a similar way, with activities slowly subsiding. Likewise, we can only speculate whether the group would have turned to a different political practice in the 1990s, when politics in Denmark turned sharply to the right and Danish troops were soon deployed in Iraq and Afghanistan.

In this book, Blekingegade Group members mention the Wollweber organization, a network of anti-fascists that operated without the official consent of communist organizations, smuggling weapons to Spain in the late 1930s and bombing ships ordered by Spain's Republican government from Danish shipyards when it looked like they would fall into the hands of Franco. The logistical framework of the Wollweber organization (the Soviet secret service) has become historically obsolete, but referencing a militant minority engaged in international anti-fascist sabotage gives us an idea of the political trajectory the Blekingegade Group members consider themselves a part of.

Among other things, the experience of fascism has taught us that at least some of the "masses" can be won for counterrevolutionary, imperialist, anti-Semitic, and racist objectives. An imperialist war in the tricont to secure superprofits or important raw materials might find support in the future as well. The left must be prepared for this and ready to act. In traditional jargon, the left needs to "organize its strategic defense." After all, the (revolutionary) left will remain a minority in the metropole for the foreseeable future.

In a certain way, the Blekingegade Group attempted to turn this necessity into a virtue. Yet, any minority sabotaging the metropolitan machinery raises important questions, too: What is at stake? (Counter)power? Hegemony? If not, what else? How high is the price? Who wins today, who tomorrow, who in a year from now? Who organizes whom? How can a social division between cadres and vanguards and "the rest" be avoided? How can protracted social isolation be prevented?

The logistical possibilities of our activities cannot be separated from the social support they enjoy. The history of the Blekingegade Group is yet another example confirming the following: when repression hits, due to errors of practice or due to a changed raison d'état, a small mishap can turn into a political disaster, namely the loss of the capacity to act. Yet, those who don't insist on denying it know that there can never be an end to global exploitation without the weakening of the imperialist metropole and the "sabotaging" of its economic, financial, and military resources. Nobody can escape the challenge posed by global necessities, despite the limited options we have.

Klaus Viehmann
Berlin, August 2013

Anti-imperialism Undercover:
An Introduction to the Blekingegade Group

Gabriel Kuhn

For acronyms of political organizations, a timeline, a list of convicted Blekingegade Group members, and currency conversion please see the appendix.

Arrests (1989)

On April 13, 1989, five people are arrested in Copenhagen as suspects in a robbery that shook Denmark six months earlier. On November 3, 1988, five men had gotten away with over thirteen million crowns after holding up a cash-in-transit vehicle at the Købmagergade post office in central Copenhagen. The heist was Denmark's most lucrative ever. It also left one person dead. With patrol cars unexpectedly arriving at the scene within less than two minutes, the robbers fired a shot from a sawed-off shotgun before making a close getaway. A pellet hit the twenty-two-year-old police officer Jesper Egtved Hansen in the eye, and he died in the hospital that same day.

Those arrested in April are Peter Døllner, Niels Jørgensen, Torkil Lauesen, Jan Weimann, and Niels Jørgensen's former girlfriend Helena.[1] The four men have been under on-and-off surveillance by the Danish intelligence service Politiets Efterretningstjeneste (PET) for almost two decades and are known communist activists with close ties to Third World liberation movements, in particular the Popular Front for the Liberation of Palestine, PFLP. It was a collaboration between PET and the Copenhagen police department that

---

1. "Helena" is a pseudonym.

made them suspects in the Købmagergade case. While Helena is released the next day, the four men remain in custody, with the police issuing an arrest warrant for yet another suspect still at large, Carsten Nielsen.

With hard evidence missing, superintendent Jørn Moos, who leads the investigation, struggles to get permission from a Copenhagen judge to keep the suspects detained. Eventually, the judge grants Moos and his team three weeks to prepare a stronger case. If they fail, the men will go free.

Producing hard evidence remains difficult, however. Thorough searches of the suspects' homes and interviews with family, friends, and coworkers remain fruitless. There is only one strong lead: identical sets of three keys found on Jørgensen, Lauesen, and Weimann. Officers test them on thousands of Copenhagen apartment doors, but with no results other than frightening unsuspecting tenants.

In the early morning hours of May 2, one day before the suspects' release date, a police patrol car north of Copenhagen receives a call about a traffic accident nearby. A single male driver has run a rented Toyota Corolla off an empty country road into a power pole. He is badly injured and unresponsive. Several items in the car, such as wigs, lock-picks, and wads of foreign cash, arouse the cops' suspicion. Alarm bells go off when the unconscious driver—who will lose his vision, his sense of smell, and his hearing in one ear as a result of the accident—is identified as Carsten Nielsen, the missing suspect in the Købmagergade case. Nielsen also carries a set of keys identical to the ones found on Jørgensen, Lauesen, and Weimann. In addition to this, the police find a bloodied telephone bill among a pile of papers on the

Blekingegade in Amager, Copenhagen, April 2013. (photo: Rebecka Söderberg)

Blekingegade 2, April 2013: the white bay belongs to the first-story apartment used by the Blekingegade Group. (photo: Rebecka Söderberg)

Toyota's backseat. It is made out to a first-story apartment at Blekingegade 2, a small and quiet street in Copenhagen's Amager district, not far from the city center.

At 3:15 PM officers arrive at Blekingegade. A couple of minutes later they have opened the apartment with the suspects' keys. This marks not only the beginning of Denmark's most captivating twentieth-century crime saga but also provides one of the most puzzling and extraordinary chapters in the history of Europe's militant anti-imperialist left of the 1970s and '80s.

The Blekingegade apartment has obviously served as a center of sophisticated criminal activity. The police find crystal radio receivers, transmitters, and antennas; masks, false beards, and state-of-the-art replicas of police uniforms; numerous false documents and machines to produce them; extensive notes outlining the Købmagergade robbery and other unlawful activities; and—in a separate room, accessible only through a hidden door—the biggest illegal weapons cache ever found in Denmark. It includes pistols, rifles, hand grenades, explosives, land mines, machine guns, and thirty-four antitank missiles. Curiously, there is also a surfboard stored in the room.

The group that had access to the Blekingegade apartment is soon dubbed *Blekingegadebanden*, the "Blekingegade Gang," or, less dramatically, *Blekingegadegruppen*, the "Blekingegade Group." According to Torkil Lauesen, the name is the result of "particularly unimaginative journalism,"[2] but it is soon established among the public and used to identify the group to this day.

---

2. From a conversation with the editor, January 2013.

Beginnings: KAK (1963–1978)

The origins of the Blekingegade Group date back to 1963, when a charismatic literary historian, Gotfred Appel, was excluded from the Moscow-loyal Communist Party of Denmark, DKP, due to his Maoist sympathies. A few months later, Appel and other disgruntled DKP members founded the first Maoist organization in Europe, namely the Kommunistisk Arbejdskreds [Communist Working Circle], KAK. KAK soon served as the official Danish sister organization of the Communist Party of China, CPC, and Appel regularly traveled to Beijing. KAK also founded the publishing house Futura, which collaborated closely with the Chinese embassy in Copenhagen, printing Maoist propaganda leaflets, the Chinese embassy's newsletter, and Mao's *Little Red Book*. KAK's own newspaper, *Orientering*, was founded in December 1963; it was renamed *Kommunistisk Orientering* in September 1964.

During the following years, Appel developed his hallmark *snylterstatsteori*, the "parasite state theory." In short, the theory claimed that the working class of the imperialist countries had become an ally of the ruling class due to its privileges in the context of the global capitalist system. Its objective interests were closer to those of Western capitalists than to those of the

Gotfred Appel meets CPC representatives in Beijing, 1964.

exploited and oppressed masses of the Third World. Therefore, the Western working class could no longer be considered a revolutionary subject. Only the masses of the Third World posed a threat to global capitalism by rebelling against the exploitation and oppression they were suffering. If their struggles were successful, the inevitable result would be a crisis of capitalism in the imperialist world, leading to the Western working class losing its privileges and being propelled back onto the revolutionary track.

The Vietnam War served as empirical evidence for Appel's theory, and in February 1965 KAK organized one of the earliest European protests against the U.S. aggression. The fact that workers remained largely absent from the demonstration—despite strong mobilization efforts at some of Copenhagen's biggest factories—seemed to confirm Appel's analysis of a corrupted and complacent Danish working class. Yet he found numerous recruits among young radicals who were drawn to KAK by the Vietnam Committee (*Vietnamkomité*) that the organization had established, its militant stance, its uniqueness among the Danish left, and not least by Appel's compelling personality.

In 1968, KAK founded a youth chapter, the Kommunistisk Ungdomsforbund [Communist Youth League], KUF, which published its own journal, *Ungkommunisten*, and initiated a group called the Anti-imperialistisk Aktionskomité [Anti-imperialist Action Committee] in order to specifically attract sympathizers in the anti-imperialist milieu.

KUF played an important role for the history of KAK and soon counted some of the men among its members who, twenty years later, would be arrested as members of the Blekingegade Group: Peter Døllner, a young carpenter, and Jan Weimann, a passionate birdwatcher and excellent chess player who had just graduated from high school, joined in 1968. Both had grown up in the Copenhagen suburb of Gladsaxe. Another early KUF member from Gladsaxe was Jan Weimann's high school friend Holger Jensen, an energetic and gregarious young man who became a driving force in both KUF and KAK. Niels Jørgensen, at the time only sixteen and still a high school student, joined in 1969. Torkil Lauesen, a medical student from Korsør, about a hundred kilometers west of Copenhagen, became a KUF member two years later.

In 1969, the relationship between KAK and the Chinese government turned sour. Gotfred Appel was not willing to make any compromises in his analysis of the European working class. When Chinese government officials hailed the European protest movements of the late 1960s, Appel criticized them relentlessly for overestimating the movements' revolutionary potential and the participation of the working class. Eventually, this led to the end of KAK's official ties to the CPC and the termination of the Futura publishing house's contract with the Chinese embassy. From this point on, KAK was no longer aligned with any political party and pursued an independent anti-imperialist course, establishing relationships with various Third World liberation movements. It didn't take long before Appel developed a particular interest in a Marxist-Leninist organization that had emerged in one of the world's most volatile regions: the Popular Front for the Liberation of Palestine, PFLP.

In 1970, Appel traveled to Jordan to meet with PFLP representatives. During the following years, several KUF members were sent to the Middle East for subsequent meetings. Members of the KUF and KAK rank and file

KUF/Anti-imperialist Action Committee poster, ca. 1969: "Without the Victory of the Third World There Will Be No Socialism Here!"

were also sent to numerous other regions in order to study the local political and economic conditions and exchange ideas with Third World liberation movements as well as anti-imperialist activists in the Western world. In Tanzania, the young Danes met representatives of FRELIMO, ZANU, and the MPLA; in Northern Ireland, Republican resistance fighters; and in Canada, members of the Liberation Support Movement, LSM.

To further strengthen the connections to African liberation movements, KAK founded the Tøj til Afrika [Clothes for Africa] project, TTA, in 1972. TTA collected clothes, tents, medicine, and money for African refugee camps administered by liberation movements. Soon, a number of TTA chapters were established around Denmark and the project provided a strong support network for KAK.

KAK itself kept a low profile in Denmark during the early 1970s. Following the protests against the World Bank congress in Copenhagen in

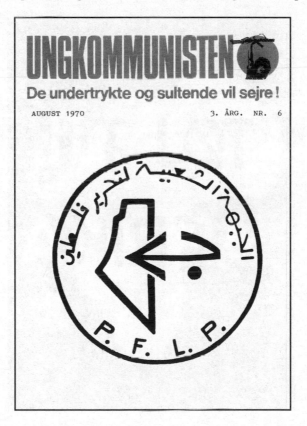

1970, during which KUF members were involved in heavy streetfighting, the organization had been targeted by security forces. Appel was furious and scolded the youngsters for their "lack of discipline" and "political immaturity," since KAK's strategy for the protests had focused on targeted militant actions rather than open confrontation with the police. As a result, KAK's focus during the next few years was on theoretical study and the formation of a disciplined organization. Appel had no plans for KAK to become a mass movement. KAK never had more than twenty-five members and was mainly considered a training ground for elite revolutionaries ready to seize the revolutionary moment in the imperialist world when it came. Outward-directed work diminished steadily. *Ungkommunisten* had ceased publication in 1970, and *Kommunistisk Orientering* was on hiatus from 1970 to 1974. In 1975, KUF was officially dissolved. The remaining members were incorporated into KAK.

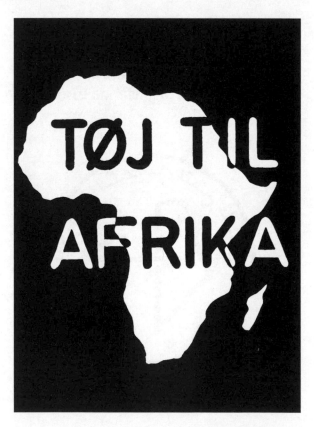

There was also another reason for KAK's low profile during the early 1970s, however. It was the period when KAK developed what was later referred to as the "illegal practice." In plain terms, this meant that robbery and fraud were used to supplement the material support for Third World liberation movements provided by Tøj til Afrika and other legal fundraising efforts. According to KAK's analysis, providing material support for Third World liberation movements was the most effective way for Western militants to support world revolution.

Only a few selected KAK members were involved in the illegal practice. The rest of the membership was not informed. Essentially, this created an inner circle within the organization that consisted of people involved in illegal activities. It was this circle that marked the beginning of the Blekingegade Group. The men arrested in April 1989 all belonged to it from the beginning.

No KAK members were ever convicted for illegal actions committed during the 1970s. Yet they remain the main suspects for a number of unresolved crimes in the greater Copenhagen area, including the 1972 burglary at a Danish Army weapons depot (weapons from the depot were discovered at the Blekingegade apartment in 1989), the 1975 robbery of a cash-in-transit truck with a take of 500,000 crowns, the 1976 robbery of a post office with a take of 550,000 crowns, and a sophisticated 1976 postal money order scam with an unsurpassed take of 1.5 million crowns. All of the crimes shared features that would also characterize the ones that the Blekingegade Group was accused of in the 1980s: highly professional execution, a lot of loot, and no traces.

After discovering the Blekingegade apartment in 1989 and reconstructing the group's history, there was much speculation about whether Gotfred Appel knew about the illegal activities of the 1970s, a fact that he sternly denied until his death in 1992. But former KAK and Blekingegade Group members speak of a tight, top-down organization in which nothing was done without the knowledge of the leadership, consisting throughout the 1970s of Appel, his partner Ulla Hauton, and the young Holger Jensen, with Jan Weimann joining in 1975.

The illegal practice—as well as all other KAK activities—came to a halt in 1977, when the organization hit a severe crisis. It started when accusations of male dominance were raised, in particular by Ulla Hauton. While Appel himself—judging from all accounts, unjustly—remained exempt from the criticism, many other male members were summoned to attend "criticism and self-criticism" sessions. Eventually, the sessions would include physical violence, with male members being expected to act as punishers in order to prove their willingness to change. A few months into what became known as the "anti–gender discrimination campaign," most KAK members, including many women, felt that the campaign had gotten out of control. Their anger now turned toward Appel and Hauton. The latter in particular was accused of manipulating the female membership due to personal and internal leadership issues. Apparently, there had been particularly strong tensions between Hauton and Holger Jensen.

At a KAK meeting on May 4, 1978, Appel and Hauton were expelled from the organization by a majority vote of the rank and file. Some days later, Appel and Hauton expelled everybody else. After much back and forth, and Appel securing the legal rights to the name *Kommunistisk Arbejdskreds*, KAK split into three factions:

1. Appel, Hauton, and a few allies continued to work under the name KAK and to publish *Kommunistisk Orientering*; two years later, the organization dissolved for good.

2. Some former KAK members formed the Marxistisk Arbejdsgruppe [Marxist Working Group], MAG, which intended to reach a new form of political practice by analyzing KAK's history. Members soon drifted away, however, and the group ceased to exist in 1980.

3. Another group of former KAK members founded the Kommunistisk Arbejdsgruppe [Communist Working Group], KA, which soon became known as Manifest–Kommunistisk Arbejdsgruppe, M-KA, named after its journal, which appeared from October 1978 to December 1982. After

FORLAGET MANIFEST, LANDSKRONAGADE 2, 2100 KØBENHAVN Ø

TLF: 01 186542   GIRO: 6 63 54 15

MANIFEST PRESS, LANDSKRONAGADE 2, 2100 COPENHAGEN, DK

TEL: 01 186542   GIRO: 6 63 54 15

that, Manifest mainly functioned as a press, publishing political books and pamphlets and printing materials for various liberation movements. Peter Døllner, Holger Jensen, Niels Jørgensen, Torkil Lauesen, and Jan Weimann all joined M-KA. None of them ever spoke to Hauton or Appel again.

In 1980, Holger Jensen died in a traffic accident when a truck hit the van he was sitting in outside a shopping center. Peter Døllner left M-KA in 1985. Jan Weimann, Niels Jørgensen, and Torkil Lauesen formed the backbone of the organization and of the Blekingegade Group until their arrests in 1989.

M-KA (1978–1989)

Ideologically, M-KA did not steer too far from KAK. It largely followed Appel's parasite state theory. However, it also added new Marxist analyses of international relations to its theoretical framework, in particular the notion of "unequal exchange" developed by the Marxist economist Arghiri Emmanuel, who argued that the discrepancies in wealth between the industrialized nations and the Third World were primarily based on imbalances in wage levels and market prices. On various occasions, M-KA members traveled to meet with the Greek-born Emmanuel in Paris, where he lived and taught. Emmanuel also contributed a preface to the 1983 M-KA book *Imperialismen idag: Det ulige bytte og mulighederne för socialisme i en delt verden* [Imperialism Today: Unequal Exchange and the Possibilities for Socialism in a Divided World], which was published in English in 1986 as *Unequal Exchange and the Prospects of Socialism*.

The main difference between M-KA and KAK was organizational. M-KA was not focused on an individual leader, allowed more internal

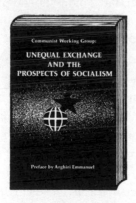

A new book on the economics of imperialism and its political consequences

Communist Working Group:
UNEQUAL EXCHANGE AND THE PROSPECTS OF SOCIALISM

Preface by Arghiri Emmanuel

from MANIFEST PRESS

debate, and was more open to collaboration with other groups of the left. M-KA remained small, never extending to more than fifteen members. Material support for Third World liberation movements remained a priority. After the turmoil during the last months of KAK, the M-KA members managed to regain the PFLP leadership's trust and reestablish contact with the other liberation movements they had collaborated with. The illegal practice continued. Once again, it was confined to an inner circle, without the rest of the membership being involved. Next to Døllner, Jørgensen, Lauesen, and Weimann, we know of three people who joined the inner circle during the 1980s. Karsten Møller Hansen, a Tøj til Afrika member from the chapter in Odense, was the first in 1982. He faded away only a few years later, but retained knowledge of most activities and contributed on occasion with small tasks. Also in 1982, Jan Weimann's younger brother Bo joined the group, working in particular on the so-called "Z-file" (Z for Zionism), a collection of data intended to help the PFLP identify Israeli agents based in Denmark. Bo left the group in 1988. The Z-file proved highly controversial when it was discovered in the Blekingegade apartment in April 1989, and the media regularly referred to it as a "Jew file." In 1987, Carsten Nielsen, a member of the Tøj til Afrika chapter in Århus, was the last one to be included in the Blekingegade Group.

Meanwhile, the core members' personal lives had undergone significant changes. Jan Weimann was married, had two children, and worked as a respected IT technician at Regnecentralen, Denmark's oldest IT company and the government's main computer service provider. His brother Bo, married with a daughter, was one of his colleagues. The Weimann brothers' families knew nothing about the illegal activities and their coworkers were in complete disbelief after the arrests, publicly doubting the police's accusations. Torkil Lauesen had been trained as medical laboratory assistant, but only worked occasionally. In 1984, his wife Lisa gave birth to a daughter. Niels Jørgensen had already become a father in 1982, when he and his girlfriend Helena had a son. Jørgensen only worked part-time and changed his jobs regularly.

When the PFLP leadership was driven from Beirut as a result of the Israeli invasion of Lebanon in 1982, the M-KA members intensified their illegal activities. Much of the PFLP's infrastructure had been destroyed and the organization was desperate for support, not least in the form of weapons.

Consequently, in November 1982, the M-KA members robbed a Swedish Army weapons depot in Flen, about a hundred kilometers west of Stockholm. The loot included numerous boxes of explosives, over a hundred hand grenades and land mines, and the thirty-four antitank missiles later found in the Blekingegade apartment.

The Blekingegade Group has also been accused of several robberies that occurred in and around Copenhagen during the following years, but none of its members has ever been convicted for any of them. The alleged crimes include a post office robbery with a take of 768,000 Danish crowns in 1982, a cash-in-transit truck robbery with a record-breaking 8.3 million take in 1983 (two Palestinian men were arrested at Charles de Gaulle Airport in Paris with 6 million Danish crowns in cash three weeks later but were never extradited to Denmark), the 1.5 million crowns robbery of a post office in 1985, and a 5.5 million heist at the Daells shopping center in central Copenhagen just before Christmas in 1906. Meanwhile, the elaborate plan to kidnap Jörn Rausing, heir to one of Sweden's wealthiest business families, was never executed. While material found in the Blekingegade apartment revealed that detailed preparations for the kidnapping had been made—including the transformation of a Norwegian summer house into a secret hideaway and demands for a ransom of twenty-five million U.S. dollars—the plan was abandoned in the summer of 1985. The episode took a heavy toll on all members. Peter Døllner left the group as a result of it.

Preparations for the group's final coup, the Købmagergade robbery, began in late 1987. According to the law enforcement agents working on the case, the group was one man short and the PFLP sent Marc Rudin, a Swiss national and longtime PFLP member, a few days before the robbery to fill the final spot.

The robbery itself went as planned. The Blekingegade Group members were on their way after exactly ninety-nine seconds, but a police patrol car had already positioned itself in the alley leading from the post office yard back to Købmagergade. Carsten Nielsen, who was driving the getaway van, managed to squeeze by, but the policemen fired a couple of shots at the vehicle. One bullet shattered the back window and got stuck in the driver's seat.

When the van turned into Købmagergade, the group spotted another patrol car behind it. Nielsen stopped the van and one of the robbers stepped out in order to fire a shot from a sawed-off shotgun. Members of the group

Købmagergade Robbery

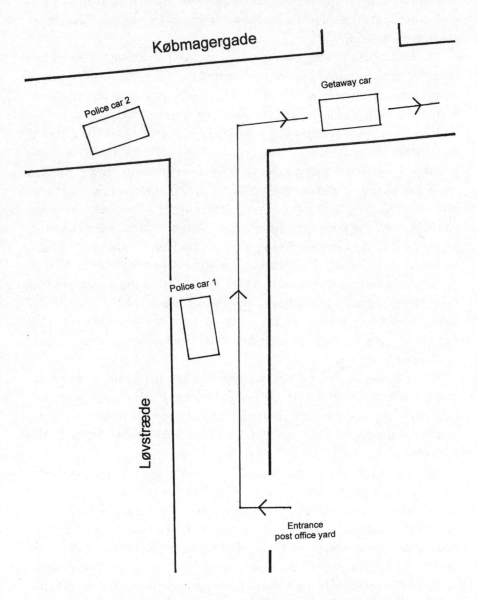

Rough sketch of the escape route after the Købmagergade robbery: the shot in the direction of police car 2 was fired when the getaway car briefly stopped at the indicated spot.

declared in court that the shot was meant to deter the police from chasing them and, ideally, to puncture the patrol car's tires. The police investigation confirmed that the shot was unaimed and fired from the hip. Most of the pellets riddled the front of a shoe store. One, however, hit the twenty-two-year-old police officer Jesper Egtved Hansen in the eye, just as he had stepped out of the car. He was rushed to hospital, where he died the same day. The robbers managed to make their escape.

The death of a policeman caused unprecedented collaboration between Danish security forces, especially the PET and the Copenhagen police department, in the search for the culprits. The collaboration would eventually lead to the arrest and sentencing of the Blekingegade Group. Prior to the Købmagergade robbery, the interest in any such collaboration was limited from all sides. During the trial it was disclosed that the group's members had been under on-and-off PET surveillance for almost two decades. The Copenhagen police department had even received tips after some of the robberies ascribed to the group, but those weren't followed up on. At the same time, PET often withheld information because the agents seemed more interested in the group's international contacts than in its domestic crimes.

The security forces' combined efforts, however, were not the only reason for the group's arrest. The members had also become increasingly negligent in security matters. Some of them have stated that if they had maintained their usual standards, there would have never been a trial. Apparently, exhaustion had caught up with the Marxist revolutionaries who had turned into Denmark's most successful criminals.

Prison (1989–1995)

Once the police had solid evidence against the men detained since April 13, 1989, more people with connections to M-KA and Tøj til Afrika were arrested. Karsten Møller Hansen on May 2, right after the discovery of the Blekingegade apartment, and Bo Weimann, Torkil Lauesen's wife Lisa, and Møller Hansen's former wife Anna on August 10.[3] Lisa and Anna were released a few weeks later. Neither was ever convicted of any crimes. Karsten

---

3. "Anna" is a pseudonym.

Møller Hansen and Bo Weimann, however, joined Døllner, Jørgensen, Lauesen, Nielsen, and Jan Weimann in the dock.

The seven were originally indicted for numerous crimes, ranging from the illegal possession of firearms and the forgery of documents to murder and terrorism. The terrorism charge was dropped before the trial even started, however, which led to speculations about the Danish authorities giving in to political pressure and the fear of PFLP reprisals. Yet, this is dismissed as sensationalism by many, including the Blekingegade Group members. At the time, the Danish antiterrorist laws could simply not sustain a terrorism charge since they only covered acts targeting the Danish state. Today, things would be different. Since the former Danish prime minister and current secretary general of NATO, Anders Fogh Rasmussen, emerged as one of Europe's staunchest supporters of the "War on Terror" in the early 2000s, Danish antiterrorist legislation has undergone dramatic changes.

The Blekingegade trial lasted eight months, from September 3, 1990, to May 2, 1991. The police and the prosecution committed many blunders, and the jury eventually acquitted the accused of most charges, most importantly murder. No individual shooter could be identified with respect to Egtved Hansen's death, and no collective intention to kill established. The jury also decided against the application of a provision in the Danish legal code that allows the increase of maximum penalties by 50 percent if the circumstances of the crime are considered particularly heinous. In the end, Jørgensen, Lauesen, Nielsen, and Jan Weimann were declared guilty of the Købmagergade robbery, Bo Weimann of compiling the Z-file, and all of the accused, including Møller Hansen and Peter Døllner, of minor violations such as the illegal possession of firearms and the forgery of documents. Jørgensen, Lauesen, and Jan Weimann were sentenced to ten years in prison, Carsten Nielsen to eight, Bo Weimann to seven, Karsten Møller Hansen to three, and Peter Døllner to one year. Møller Hansen and Døllner were released on the spot (it is common in Denmark to be released after two thirds of the sentence). Bo Weimann and Carsten Nielsen were released in April 1994, Jørgensen, Lauesen, and Jan Weimann in December 1995. The last three had been especially active in prisoners' rights issues during their time behind bars.

Marc Rudin was arrested on October 14, 1991, by a Turkish border patrol and accused of entering the country illegally from Syria. He was extradited to

Denmark in October 1993, where he was sentenced to eight years in prison for his alleged participation in the Købmagergade robbery. He was deported to Switzerland in February 1997 and remains barred from entering Denmark.

Aftermath

The Blekingegade Group's story has been captivating Denmark for over twenty years. Attention has been particularly strong in recent years, mainly due to the 2007 release of a two-volume, eight-hundred-page history of the group titled *Blekingegadebanden* and authored by the acclaimed journalist Peter Øvig Knudsen. The book sold 350,000 copies in Denmark, which made it one of the country's most successful nonfiction books ever. It has been translated into Swedish, Norwegian, and (in an abridged version) German. In 2008, a one-volume "luxury edition" was published, including numerous original documents from the police files. Bo Weimann was the only former Blekingegade Group member who agreed to be interviewed by Øvig Knudsen. He was also the main protagonist of a 2009 documentary film titled *Blekingegadebanden*. Meanwhile, the journalists Anders-Peter Mathiasen and Jeppe Facius published two books in collaboration with the chief investigator in the Blekingegade case, Jørn Moos: *Blekingegadebetjenten krim- inalinspektør Jørn Moos fortæller* [The Blekingegade Cop: Superintendent Jørn Moos Tells His Story] (2007) collects stories from Moos's professional life, while *Politiets hemmeligheder: Kriminalinspektør Jørn Moos genåbner Blekingegadesagen* [Secrets of the Police: Superintendent Jørn Moos Reopens the Blekingegade Case] (2009) focuses on the complicated relationship between the Danish police and PET—it also provided the basis for the 2010 documentary film *Blekingegade—sagen genoptaget* [Blekingegade: The Case Reopened]. In January 2009, the play *Blekingegade*, written by Claus Flygare, opened at Husets Teater in Copenhagen, and in the winter of 2009–2010, the TV series *Blekingegade*—quite openly blending fact and fiction—aired on public Danish television.

About This Book

This book was largely motivated by the portrayal of the Blekingegade Group in mainstream media.

In 2008, Niels Jørgensen, Torkil Lauesen, and Jan Weimann wrote an article titled "Det handler om politik" (translated in this volume as "It Is All About Politics") in response to Øvig Knudsen's book. The article was published in a Blekingegade Group special of the Danish left-wing periodical *Social Kritik* in March 2009. A slightly revised version appeared on the website www.snylterstaten.dk shortly after. "It Is All About Politics" tells the story of the Blekingegade Group from the perspective of its longest-standing members and constitutes the first part of this book. The version included here has been adapted to an international audience in collaboration with Torkil Lauesen and Jan Weimann; Niels Jørgensen died in September 2008. Passages requiring a profound knowledge of Danish society, politics, and law, or a reading of Øvig Knudsen's work have been omitted.

The book's second part consists of an extended interview with Torkil Lauesen and Jan Weimann, conducted in the spring of 2013. The interview includes additional information on the group's history and discussions about current socialist and internationalist politics.

The book's third part brings together several historical documents: a 1966 essay by Gotfred Appel titled "Socialism and the Bourgeois Way of Life," KAK and M-KA self-presentations, and the chapter "What Can Communists in the Imperialist Countries Do?" from the M-KA book *Unequal Exchange and the Prospects of Socialism.*

The preface by Klaus Viehmann was originally written for the German edition, published by Unrast Verlag. All translations were done by the editor.

The intention behind this book is to contribute to left-wing movement history. The activities of the Blekingegade Group constitute one of the most unique chapters of radical socialist and anti-imperialist politics in Europe during the 1970s and 1980s. While a number of secondary sources have been published, most notably Øvig Knudsen's study, none of the material has been made available in English. Furthermore, even in the Nordic languages a book featuring the recollections and reflections of the group's key members has been missing. As an editor, I have seen my role as providing a space in which these recollections and reflections can be expressed. Their political evaluation is left to the reader.

I would like to thank Poul Mikael Allarp, a former KAK and MAG member who maintains the website www.snylterstaten.dk, and Torkil Lauesen and Jan Weimann for their collaboration during this project and for providing valuable material from KAK's and M-KA's history. Today, Torkil Lauesen works for the city of Copenhagen in a neighborhood renewal project and regularly contributes to left-wing journals. On the basis of his prison experiences, he has also written the book *Fra forbedringshus til parkeringshus—magt og modmagt i Vridsløselille Statsfængsel* [From Rehabilitation to Warehousing: Power and Counterpower in the Vridsløselille State Prison] (1998) and the prisoners' manual *Att leva i fängelse—en överlevnadshandbok för fånger* [Life in Prison: A Survival Manual for Prisoners] (2000). Jan Weimann works at a Copenhagen job center which tries to find work for the unemployed. He still enjoys watching birds and checkmating the king.

Niels, Lisa, and Torkil in Paris, 1982.

It Is All About Politics

Niels Jørgensen, Torkil Lauesen, and Jan Weimann

INTRODUCTION

Preface

The first draft of this article was finished in May 2008. It was written by Jan Weimann, Niels Jørgensen, and Torkil Lauesen, who have been called the "inner circle" of the Blekingegade Group. All three of us were sentenced to ten years in prison for criminal activities motivated by supporting Third World liberation movements.

In September 2008, Niels Jørgensen died after a few days of sickness. This was a huge personal loss for us. It also made it difficult to finish the article. Yet, we decided to do so nonetheless, not least because Niels would have wanted us to.

Niels Jørgensen remains listed as a coauthor because the article's contents have not changed since his passing and because he clearly left his mark on the text.

Torkil Lauesen and Jan Weimann
Copenhagen, January 20, 2009

The Article's Intention

For the past few years, there has been extensive media coverage of the so-called Blekingegade Gang. Especially the journalist Peter Øvig Knudsen (PØK) and the retired police investigator Jørn Moos have made regular media appearances as a result of their books about the Blekingegade Group. In early 2009, both the documentary film *Blekingegadebanden* and the play *Blekingegade* premiered. A TV series produced by Zentropa is on its way.[1]

PØK's two-volume work is widely regarded as the truth about the Blekingegade Group. Together with Moos's books, it might well be considered the authoritative source on the subject in the future. We find this unsettling. The current media coverage of the Blekingegade Group is full of distortions and wrong assumptions. The aforementioned publications have significantly contributed to this. At least in part, this article is a response to them.

The name "Blekingegade Gang" is a label created by the media. We saw ourselves first and foremost as a political group. All of us have been politically interested and organized since a young age. In the beginning of the 1970s, we became members of the Kommunistisk Arbejdskreds, KAK. The original KAK dissolved in 1978. Afterward, the three of us were cofounders of Manifest–Kommunistisk Arbejdsgruppe, M-KA.

In this text, we want to outline the political practice of both organizations. A part of this practice was to secure material support for Third World liberation movements by illegal means. The practice did not involve all of the organizations' members. It was pursued by a "subgroup," whose membership fluctuated and who will be referred to here as the "Blekingegade Group."

The intention of the article is therefore twofold:

1. We feel a need to outline our political project.
In the 1970s and '80s, when we were politically active, the world looked very different from the way it does today. This is why the article includes a description of the era. How did we see the world when we developed our political project? What were our positions and theories? Who were we inspired by? Who were our partners and allies? Why did we choose to act the way we did?

---

1. Zentropa is a Danish film company founded in 1992 by Lars von Trier and Peter Aalbæk Jensen. The TV series, entitled *Blekingegade*, aired in late 2009 and early 2010. Regarding the documentary film and the play, see the introduction. —Ed.

2. We want to correct wrong assumptions about our theory and practice.
We do not intend to systematically address all the wrong assumptions that have been made about our political perspectives, the people and organizations we worked with, and our legal as well as illegal activities. But we want to address some of the most important ones and some of the most common misunderstandings and misrepresentations.

Øvig's Sources and Methods

PØK's primary sources are police reports. The people he talked to were mostly law enforcement agents. When he was interviewed by dk4 in the old Horsens State Prison for the program *Litteratursiden* [The Literary Page],[2] PØK confirmed that he went through the police files under the guidance of police officers. Apparently, the files would have been impossible to make sense of otherwise. However, it seems to us that he never even bothered to double-check on most of the information he received. He appears to have taken most of the police's guesswork for facts. PØK also admitted in the program that the suspense factor was very important for his book. This obviously compromised the documentary quality. It is therefore not surprising that PØK arrived at plenty of wrong conclusions. We will address the most problematic ones on the following pages.

We ourselves want to focus on politics rather than crime. After all, the Blekingegade case was about politics. We also look at what happened in the context of its time, while PØK's approach is characterized by the current obsession with "terrorism."

Both PØK's research and his political knowledge have clear limitations. It is clear, for example, that he has not even looked at some of the most crucial material, such as the journals, pamphlets, and books published by KAK and M-KA. His knowledge of liberation movements hardly goes beyond that of glossy magazine articles. Proper research would have provided answers to many of his questions and prevented many of his false conclusions. The most serious problem, however, is that it is impossible for his readers to distinguish fact from fiction. PØK's work lacks references for almost any of the claims he makes. Readers can therefore not establish the credibility of his book's contents.

---

2. The Danish television channel dk4 was launched in 1994. —Ed.

OUR THEORY, PRACTICE, AND ALLIES

The first section of the article addresses four topics:

1. KAK's origins and the development of its political theory, that is, the "parasite state theory."
2. KAK's legal and illegal practice.
3. Our relationship to the PFLP and our reasons for not having any connections to the German Red Army Faction, RAF, and Wadi Haddad's Special Operations.[3]
4. The split within KAK and the founding of M-KA.

KAK and Our Political Origins

In order to understand the background of our political practice it is necessary to describe KAK, the organization in which we received our political schooling.

This description entails:

- ► a short overview of KAK's history and theory, with a particular focus on the international political framework in which the organization was formed
- ► the organizational characteristics of KAK, which had two objectives: one, to form an effective political group, and two, to make a small contribution to undermining imperialism by supporting strategically selected liberation movements
- ► a rejection of the claim that KAK was a Maoist organization throughout the 1970s
- ► a rejection of our portrayal as politically isolated dreamers, when our political worldview was shared by many movements and theorists who we were in constant contact with

---

3. The group was also known under the names "External Operations" and "Special Operations Group." —Ed.

> ► an explanation for why KAK chose an illegal political practice in addition to a legal one

KAK was founded in 1964 by former members of the Danish Communist Party, DKP. The early KAK leadership consisted of seven people, including Gotfred Appel and Benito Scocozza.[4] KAK's journal was named *Kommunistisk Orientering*. After its foundation, KAK published a twelve-point program, in which it criticized the DKP and the Soviet Union.[5] KAK's members were strongly inspired by Mao and the Communist Party of China, CPC.

In addition to the Maoist orientation, KAK had a strong internationalist outlook and was the first organization in Denmark to call for a demonstration against the Vietnam War. The demonstration was held on February 8, 1965, under the slogan, "Free the South, Defend the North, Reunite the Fatherland!" The same year, KAK took the initiative to collect money for a leprosy sanatorium in North Vietnam. This lay the foundation for the support of liberation movements that later became the organization's focus. KAK thought that the fight against American imperialism would undermine the capitalist system and bring us closer to socialism. In 1966, KAK founded the Vietnam Committee (Vietnamkomité), which turned into a broad social movement.

Soon, however, KAK experienced internal conflict. Members were divided in their evaluation of the Danish working class's revolutionary potential. As a result, Benito Scocozza and others left. This made KAK a more united and focused organization, but also a smaller one. The remaining members were convinced that the fight for Vietnam's liberation was the most important struggle for socialists, even in Denmark.

KAK published an increasing number of articles explaining the difficulties in mobilizing Danish workers for international solidarity. Its analysis was that the Danish working class had been "bribed" with high wages. In 1966, the essence of what was later called the "parasite state theory" was outlined in a *Kommunistisk Orientering* article. The article emphasized the

---

4. In 1968, Benito Scocozza cofounded the Maoist KFML. He served as its chairman until 1975, and as the chairman of its successor, KAP, until 1984. (For KFML/KAP, see the appendix.) —Ed.

5. KAK, *Til alle kommunister! Till alle der vil socialisme* [To All Communists! To All Who Want Socialism] (Copenhagen: Futura, 1964).

consequences of the theory for socialists in the rich countries: "If we want socialism to become a reality in the Western capitalist world, including Denmark, then it is our highest duty to support oppressed nations and peoples in their fight against Western capitalism, the common enemy."[6]

In 1968, KAK founded the youth organization Kommunistisk Ungdomsforbund, KUF, which published the journal *Ungkommunisten*. KAK was still small and wanted to attract young activists. One of KUF's first initiatives was the founding of the Anti-imperialist Action Committee (Anti-imperialistisk Aktionskomité).

Only at this point did we personally enter the picture. None of us was part of KAK's early history. Jan Weimann first established ties to KAK in 1967 during a demonstration against the Greek military junta. Niels Jørgensen joined the organization in 1969 after meeting KUF members during protests against the Copenhagen screening of *The Green Berets*, a film glorifying U.S. war crimes in Vietnam. Torkil Lauesen joined KUF in 1971. Holger Jensen, who received much attention in PØK's book, became the leader of the Anti-imperialist Action Committee.

By 1968, KAK was led by Gotfred Appel and his partner Ulla Hauton. The parasite state theory became increasingly important for the organization.[7] Its essence was that the rich (imperialist) countries exploited the countries of the Third World, mainly in the form of "superprofits" extracted as a result of foreign direct investments. The superprofits not only made Western capitalists richer but also increased the wages of the Western working class, which now no longer had "only its chains to lose."[8] Western workers now also had an objective interest in defending global capitalism, since the system guaranteed them disproportionately high wages. It was crystal-clear to us that the Western European working class was not revolutionary in the 1960s—you just had to take a good look around you. This realization became our starting point. It defined, in a nutshell, the parasite state theory.

---

6. KAK, *Perspektiverne for socialisme i Danmark* [Perspectives for Socialism in Denmark], insert in *Kommunistisk Orientering* nos. 3–5, 1966.

7. See also KAK, *To linjer* [Two lines], insert in *Kommunistisk Orientering* no. 18, 1968, to no. 2, 1969.

8. See Karl Marx and Friedrich Engels, *The Communist Manifesto* (1848), http://www.marxists.org/archive/marx/works/1848/communist-manifesto/ch04.htm.

When Appel and Hauton added the final touches to the parasite state theory in 1968, KAK was still the official Danish ally of the CPC and owned the exclusive rights to the Danish edition of Mao's *Little Red Book*.

From Maoism to Anti-imperialism

When the CPC held its Ninth National Congress in 1969, some of its declarations sounded as if the revolution in Western Europe would break out any minute. Its description of the Western European working class as "revolutionary" was a complete delusion. KAK criticized this in a special issue of *Kommunistisk Orientering*. As a result, the official ties to the CPC were cut.

A look at the texts published in *Kommunistisk Orientering* during the 1970s makes it clear that KAK was no longer a Maoist organization. The issues from 1974 and 1975[9] include a description of KAK's politics, a critique of Scocozza, a critique of the German RAF, a contribution by Don Barnett,[10] and articles on socialist theory, the famine in India, multinational oil companies, the West German working class, and U.S. agricultural policies. Not a single article talks about China. The fact that KAK was hoping for China to build a socialist state without repeating the mistakes of the Soviet Union under Stalin does not mean that KAK was Maoist. It is therefore incorrect when PØK and others speak of KAK as a Maoist organization during that time. The members of KFML/KAP, led by Benito Scocozza, took on the role of being China's supporters in Denmark. PØK belonged to the organization for some time, so he should know this.

Let us summarize:

- ▸ KAK's political line differed in many ways from that of the CPC.
- ▸ We had a completely different analysis of the Western working class.
- ▸ KAK considered it crucial to support Third World liberation movements, while for the CPC the decisive struggle was the one of the Western working class.

---

9. No *Kommunistisk Orientering* issues were published between 1970 and 1974—see also the introduction. —Ed.

10. Don Barnett was the founder of the LSM (see the appendix). —Ed.

▶ We had completely different perspectives on the Soviet Union: while we saw the Soviet Union as a tactical ally in the fight against imperialism (even if we didn't see eye to eye with them on everything, especially not the political implementation of socialism), the CPC saw the Soviet Union as the most dangerous imperialist power of them all.[11]

"What Is the Situation in Western Europe?" *Kommunistisk Orientering* special issue, May 1969.

---

11. Our views on the Soviet Union were summarized in the pamphlet *Myter om Sovjet* [Myths about the Soviet Union], authored by M.K. Andersen and T. Retbøll (Copenhagen: Manifest, 1986).

Basically all of the Third World movements we supported were criticized by the CPC and the Maoist organizations in Western Europe. Most Maoist organizations supported other movements; movements we had no sympathies for whatsoever. In Angola, for example, we supported the MPLA, while China supported UNITA and FNLA. UNITA was a group of anticommunist bandits who terrorized the civil population. By supporting them, China formed an alliance with the U.S., South Africa, and Israel. Later they also collaborated with the FNLA, which was known for murdering everyone when attacking white farms: the white owners as well as the black workers and their families. In the Middle East, the Chinese approach was also different from ours. The PFLP never received any support from China other than a box full of Mao books.

For younger generations, the differences between the socialist organizations of the 1970s might amount to little more than choosing different chiefs. For those of us who were active at the time, however, these differences were crucial. It was important that we were not Maoists, because we fundamentally disagreed with China's foreign policy. Our reference points were the unjustified exploitation and oppression of the Third World and the sympathies we had for the revolutionary movements emerging there as a consequence of this.

In our analysis, the Marxist concept of "contradiction" played a central role. In short, a contradiction consists of two forces opposing one another and being dependent on one another at the same time. Traditional Marxist literature focuses on the contradiction between capitalists and workers. For us, the main contradiction was the one between the poor/exploited countries and the rich/imperialist ones. On the basis of the parasite state theory, we saw the contradiction between workers and capitalists in the Western world mitigated; they shared a common short-term interest, namely the increase of profits made from Third World exploitation (even if there was a constant struggle over the profits' distribution, mainly expressed in wage disputes).

For us, the Third World was the focal point. It was in the Third World where social mass movements emerged and political organizations took up arms to overthrow the local elites and to end imperialist exploitation. We saw it as our main task to support these movements and organizations in their struggle.

Unity with Third World Liberation Movements

We were not alone in our analysis, even if it was not especially popular among the Danish left. The Third World liberation movements we collaborated with shared our views. We had the same goals: to liberate the Third World from imperialism; to end economic exploitation; and to move in a socialist direction. Che Guevara, one of the leaders during the Cuban Revolution, and later Cuba's foreign minister, famously spoke of creating "many Vietnams":

> How close and bright would the future appear if two, three, many Vietnams flowered on the face of the globe, with their quota of death and their immense tragedies, with their daily heroism, with their repeated blows against imperialism, forcing it to disperse its forces under the lash of the growing hatred of the peoples of the world![12]

Our support for Third World liberation movements had both a short-term and a long-term goal. The short-term goal was to help establish Third World countries' economic and political self-determination. The long-term goal was to diminish the superprofits of the imperialist countries' capitalists and to thereby give new urgency to the contradiction between these countries' capitalist and working classes. As a consequence, socialism would become a possibility even in our part of the world. Many Third World leaders and revolutionaries shared this perspective. Jawaharlal Nehru, India's first prime minister, wrote the following already in 1933:

> It is said that capitalism managed to prolong its life to our day because of a factor which perhaps Marx did not fully consider. This was the exploitation of colonial empires by the industrial countries of the West. This gave fresh life and prosperity to it, at the expense, of course, of the poor countries so exploited.[13]

---

12. Ernesto (Che) Guevara, "Vietnam and the World Struggle for Freedom," quoted from George Lavan (ed.), *Che Guevara Speaks* (New York: Pathfinder, 1967), 159.

13. Jawaharlal Nehru, *Glimpses of World History* (Delhi: Oxford University Press, 1982 [1934]), 548.

Che Guevara wrote in 1965:

> Ever since monopoly capital took over the world, it has kept
> the greater part of humanity in poverty, dividing all the profits
> among the group of the most powerful countries. The standard
> of living in those countries is based on the extreme poverty in
> our countries. To raise the living standards of the underdevel-
> oped nations, therefore, we must fight against imperialism.[14]

Julius K. Nyerere, at the time the president of Tanzania, compared the conditions of the nineteenth-century European working class with the labor force
of the poor nations in 1973:

> The only difference between the two situations is that the ben-
> eficiaries in the international situation now are the national
> economies of the rich nations—which includes the working
> class of those nations. And the disagreements about division
> of the spoils, which used to exist between members of the capi-
> talist class in the nineteenth century, are now represented by
> disagreement about the division of the spoils between workers
> and capitalists in the rich economies.[15]

Not only politicians shared our analysis. Also numerous scholars did. Eric
Hobsbawm, one of the world's most renowned historians, wrote about the
connection between imperialism and the labor aristocracy in 1964:

> The roots of British reformism no doubt lie in the history of a
> century of economic world supremacy, and the creation of a
> labour aristocracy, or even more generally, of an entire working
> class which drew advantages from it.[16]

---

14. Ernesto (Che) Guevara, "Speech at the Afro-Asian Conference in Algeria,"
February 24, 1965, http://www.marxists.org/archive/guevara/1965/02/24.htm.

15. Julius K. Nyerere, "A Call to European Socialists" (November 1972), quoted from
Nyerere, *Freedom and Development: A Selection from Writings and Speeches 1968–
1973* (Dar es Salaam: Oxford University Press, 1973), 374–75.

16. Eric Hobsbawm, *Labouring Men* (London: Weidenfeld and Nicolson, 1964), 341.

In 1970, the respected economist Joan Robinson stated the following:

> It was not only superior productivity that caused capitalist wealth to grow. The whole world was ransacked for resources. The dominions overseas that European nations had been acquiring and fighting over since the sixteenth century, and others also, were now greatly developed to supply raw materials to industry. ... The industrial workers at home gained from imperialism in three ways. First of all, raw materials and foodstuffs were cheap relatively to manufactures which maintained the purchasing power of their wages. Tea, for instance, from being a middle-class luxury became an indispensable necessity for the English poor. Secondly the great fortunes made in industry, commerce and finance spilled over to the rest of the community in taxes and benefactions while continuing investment kept the demand for labour rising with the population. ... Finally, lording it around the world as members of the master nations, they could feed their self-esteem upon notions of racial superiority. ... Thus the industrial working class, while apparently struggling against the system, was in fact absorbed in it.[17]

The Political Situation in the 1970s

While the revolutionary perspectives in Western Europe seemed to decline, the situation in the Third World looked promising, as the rebellion against imperialism and colonialism was on the rise everywhere. There were many possible reasons for a liberation struggle emerging in a particular place. The wish for national independence—*the national aspect*—was one. The wish for food on the table and for breaking the power of a foreign ruling class as well as the exploitation of resources and labor by foreign corporations—*the economic aspect*—was another. The wish for fundamental changes to power relations and the distribution of resources within the country—*the socialist aspect*—was a third. Often, two or all three of them were interrelated.

---

17. Joan Robinson, *Freedom and Necessity* (London: George Allen & Unwin, 1970), 64–66.

◆ *The national aspect*

The national movements wanted to end the political domination of foreign powers. Their objective was decolonization. On the African continent, Algeria achieved liberation from France in 1962. There was a national liberation struggle in Eritrea. There were uprisings in the Portuguese colonies of Mozambique, Angola, Guinea-Bissau, and the Cape Verde Islands. The national aspect was also strong in countries where the political power was in the hands of a white minority. In Rhodesia (today's Zimbabwe), a national liberation struggle was waged against Ian Smith's settler regime. There was a liberation struggle in South-West Africa (today's Namibia), and the struggle against the apartheid regime in South Africa. In the Middle East, the Palestinian liberation movement grew rapidly, and in Turkey, the Kurdish minority rose up in protest.

◆ *The economic aspect*

There were uprisings in many of the countries in which people experienced particularly severe forms of exploitation and oppression. People who had nothing to lose (workers, peasants, slum dwellers, etc.) fought against feudal and capitalist regimes that were often dependent on foreign powers. There was revolutionary unrest in Morocco. In Ethiopia, Emperor Hailo Selassie was ousted in a coup in 1974. In Iran, people rebelled against the Shah. Latin America experienced a wave of rebellions and social change. Fidel Castro seized power in Cuba in 1959. Salvador Allende was elected head of state in a democratic election in Chile in 1970. Strong liberation movements were active in Guatemala, Nicaragua, and El Salvador. Latin America was known as the backyard of the CIA, which supported the most corrupt and brutal regimes. In many countries, death squads tortured and killed dissidents, whether they were oppositional politicians, unionists, or revolutionary Catholic priests.

◆ *The socialist aspect*

Numerous liberation movements had a socialist ideology similar to KAK's. The socialist perspective of the Vietnamese revolution affected liberation movements in other Asian countries, especially in Cambodia and Laos, while new communist movements were emerging in Thailand and in the

Philippines. In South Yemen, a left-wing leadership had seized power, while a liberation movement was gaining strength in Oman.

◆ *The struggle was global and the prospects were bright*
Undoubtedly, the Vietnamese Front National de Liberté, FNL, was responsible for much of the optimism with which we, and others, approached Third World liberation struggles. The FNL had been founded in South Vietnam in 1960 and, with the support of the North, it had been fighting for fifteen years for a free and united Vietnam. The struggle was directed against the ruling South Vietnamese elite and its foreign allies, first France and then the U.S. The goal was to create a united socialist nation. This became a reality after Saigon was conquered on April 30, 1975. The FNL knew—and proved—that it was possible to stand up against any force, even if it was as powerful as the U.S. army.

Several new nations with socialist promise were established as a result of successful liberation struggles at the time. In the mid-1970s, you could cover the entire world map with red pins if you used one for every active liberation movement. The struggle in the Third World was real. It was no fantasy.[18]

◆ *The role of the USA*
The uprisings were centered in the Third World, but rebellious movements were also emerging in the U.S. The black struggle for equal rights made headlines around the world every day. Demonstrations against government policies gathered thousands of people. Some political groups seemed to prepare for open struggle; we are thinking particularly of the Black Muslims and the Black Panther Party for Self-Defense.

The Black Panthers were founded in 1966 by Huey P. Newton, Bobby Seale, and others. One of their objectives was to protect the black community from police brutality. Therefore they armed themselves for self-defense, which, as we know, is legal in the U.S. In 1968, their newspaper had a print-run of five

---

18. For an analysis of the development of national liberation struggles, see also Torkil Lauesen, "Den nationale befrielseskamps problemer" [The Problems of the National Liberation Struggle], 3 parts, *Gaia* nos. 61–63, 2008–2009.

hundred thousand. Very soon, the organization was brutally and systematically crushed by the American state. The police attacked one Panther office
after another and killed many of the movement's members, including some
of its most prominent leaders. As a result, many Panthers were forced to go
underground or flee the country.

In 1969, there also appeared a militant group of white socialists, the
Weather Underground, who, in opposition to the war in Vietnam, committed acts of sabotage against government offices and the American weapons
industry.

None of this meant that a revolution in the U.S. was waiting around the
corner. But it showed that even the U.S. was fragile. It seemed that if the flow
of wealth from the poor countries to the U.S. could be stopped, the country
would experience a crisis that would not be solved by a few simple reforms.

In short, in the late 1960s and the early 1970s, there was a real possibility—a "window"—for radical global change. We saw the combination of
anti-colonial and anti-imperialist struggles in many parts of the Third World
and the anti-authoritarian youth revolt in Europe as the objective conditions
for such a change to not only be possible, but probable. This contributed to
our radicalization and commitment as militants. We were not just pursuing
a dream. It seemed possible for us to be a small wheel in a big revolutionary
process.

◆ *Political studies*
The study of Marxism, that is, the study of historical materialism and political economy, was very important for us. It made us understand how the
world's forces related to one another. It was important for us that our practice be based on theory as well as empirical analysis, and not just on wishful
thinking. We wanted to understand the patterns of economic exchange and
the fabric of social relations. We considered this mandatory for being able
to effectively change the world. A lot of time went into studying Karl Marx's
Capital. We also conducted economic analysis as well as in-depth political
studies of various countries, and examined the liberation movements we
considered collaborating with. In all of this, a purely theoretical perspective
was never enough. KAK members embarked on many travels in the early
1970s to get a better understanding of what life was like in different parts

of the world. Each journey lasted up to a few months. The experiences were summarized in reports about economic conditions, power relations, living standards, imperialist dependencies, etc. The reports were then discussed at KAK meetings. The countries we visited were India, Iraq, Iran, Syria, Israel, Lebanon, Egypt, Tanzania, Kenya, and the Western countries of Portugal, Germany, Northern Ireland, the USA, and Canada.

Our studies seemed to confirm that the revolutionary potential lay in the Third World where capitalism produced the value it needed to retain its momentum and where objective reasons (exploitation and oppression) existed for radical resistance to emerge.

The Western European working class desired higher wages and stronger welfare. It did not desire radical change. This implies no moral judgment. It was a simple matter of interests. Our analysis corresponded to our own experiences. In the late 1960s and early 1970s, many KAK members worked at big companies: B&W, FLSmidth, Tuborg, and others.[19] In the mid-1970s, four KAK members also worked in Germany for a year to get an impression of the situation in a different Western European country.

Today, we believe that history has proven our analysis right. Since the 1970s, the Western European working class has not shown any desire for revolutionary change. We were not the dreamers; we were the realists. It wasn't us but the DKP and KAP who wrote socialist programs for Denmark.

In Marxism, one distinguishes between a revolution's object and subject. The object is the economic and political conditions you wish to change. The subject is the oppressed and exploited social groups that can make this change possible. In traditional Marxist theory, it is the working class that occupies the role of the revolutionary subject. However, we did not see the Western working class as such, since its situation was not defined by exploitation and oppression, at least not primarily. On the contrary, Western European workers had much to lose: their living standards were high; many working-class families owned a house and a car. There was no desire for revolution. The situation was entirely different for workers and peasants in Third World countries. It is wrong to say that we substituted ourselves—or

---

19. Burmeister & Wain (B&W) was a big Danish shipyard (closed 1980), FLSmidth is a major international machine manufacturer, and Tuborg is one of Europe's biggest breweries. —Ed.

a small group of militants—for the working class. The people we saw as the revolutionary subject were the ones active in Third World movements with popular support.

If a revolutionary movement wants to be successful it needs a population that is both tired of the old political system and disillusioned with democratic solutions. Marx spoke of a class that had nothing to lose "but its chains":

> The Communists disdain to conceal their views and aims. They openly declare that their ends can be attained only by the forcible overthrow of all existing social conditions. Let the ruling classes tremble at a Communistic revolution. The proletarians have nothing to lose but their chains. They have a world to win. Working men of all countries, unite![20]

We found meaning in our political work, because we saw a correlation between our theoretical studies and our practical experiences. Our political commitment was based on the analysis of an unequal world, the understanding of imperialist exploitation, and first-hand experiences in the Third World. Our goal was to contribute to the struggle of Third World people for a better life. The terrible working and living conditions and the political oppression that many of them suffered peaked in the assassinations of union members and militants fighting for social change. This had a big impact on us.

◆ *We were not isolated*

Many on the Danish left have described us as politically isolated. Bente Hansen, for example, wrote in the journal *Salt*:

> The author [PØK] has done everything he could—especially in his many interviews—to make the group appear as an "integrated part of the left." Ironically, his book proves the exact opposite: by the time the group really became active (1969–1970), it was already revolving entirely around itself and had rejected

---

20. Karl Marx and Friedrich Engels, *The Communist Manifesto* (1848), http://www.marxists.org/archive/marx/works/1848/communist-manifesto/ch04.htm.

the rest of the left. As a result, it never had a solid place in the left either. The group's obscurity largely has to be blamed on its own members. They mistrusted the left and had a deep contempt for what they derogatorily called the "left-wing mush."[21]

It is true that our approach was not popular within the Danish left and that it was regarded as bizarre. However, being isolated within the Danish left does not mean that we were isolated in general. We strongly reject the notion that we had no political discussions with other militants or that we were completely detached from popular movements. We simply had discussions with people and movements that usually were not from Denmark—and if they were, then they were not members of the DKP, KAP, or Venstresocialisterne [Left Socialists].[22] We discussed politics with liberation movements whenever we visited them or whenever some of their representatives came to Denmark. We also had contacts to Western political groups that shared our perspectives and political priorities, such as the Liberation Support Movement, LSM, in North America and like-minded groups in Norway and Sweden. In Denmark we had contacts with solidarity projects supporting the PFLOAG/PFLO in Oman and movements in the Philippines, the Western Sahara, and El Salvador. Through Tøj til Afrika we were in contact with Ulandsklunserne[23] and other organizations providing practical help for refugee camps, among them WUS (the later Ibis)[24] and Mellemfolkelig Samvirke.[25] We felt in no way isolated.

---

21. Bente Hansen, "Mossad og Blekingegade" [Mossad and Blekingegade], *Salt* no. 2, April 2007, 28. *Salt* is a bimonthly journal for "social, political, and cultural issues," founded in 1992. "Left-wing mush" is an approximate translation of *venstredynen*, a *dyne* being a blanket or a soft, shapeless object; according to a Danish saying, *Det er som at slå i en dyne*, an action that doesn't give any results is "like hitting a *dyne*"; this is what KAK members accused the rest of the Danish left of. The common Danish name used for the left is *venstrefløjen*, literally, "the left wing." —Ed.

22. Venstresocialisterne is a small leftist party founded in 1967. Today, they are part of the 1989-founded Enhedslisten–De Rød-Grønne [Red-Green Alliance], together with the DKP and the Trotskyist *Socialistisk Arbejderparti* [Socialist Workers Party]. KAP also belonged to the Red-Green Alliance before disbanding in 1994. —Ed.

23. *Ulandsklunserne* roughly translates as "ragpickers for developing countries"; it was a collective involved in Third World solidarity projects. —Ed.

KAK's Practice

The decision to support liberation movements both morally and materially was made early on in KAK's history. It was considered the most important revolutionary contribution a socialist organization in the imperialist world could make. The material support we provided was based on both legal and illegal activities.

In its political practice, KAK had two goals. The first one was to create a disciplined and effective organization able to work both legally and, under certain circumstances, illegally. The second one was to exercise political and practical solidarity with Third World liberation movements.

Gotfred Appel and Ulla Hauton wanted to develop a communist group that had the will and the ability to partake in activities they considered necessary; this could mean to set militant examples in demonstrations or to engage in illegal actions. Here are some examples:

In May 1969, Copenhagen's Saga cinema announced a screening of *The Green Berets*, an American propaganda film about the war in Vietnam. All across Western Europe screenings of the film had been prevented by demonstrations. Together with other groups on the left, KAK decided to prevent the one in Denmark. The Anti-imperialist Action Committee and KUF ended up on the frontlines of the Saga protests. They doused the seats of the cinema with butyric acid and gave the demonstrations a militant character. After several days of rioting between left-wing activists and an alliance of police officers and members of the motorcycle club *De Vilde Engle* [The Wild Angels], the screening was canceled.

In September 1970, the World Bank held a congress in Copenhagen. Many on the left considered the World Bank a tool for the imperialist exploitation of the Third World. KAK participated in the protests with the objective

---

24. WUS Denmark was the Danish branch of the international World University Service, originally an organization focusing on human rights and education. The Danish branch was founded in 1966 and focused strongly on supporting social movements and activists in the Third World. In 1991, it left the international organization and changed its name to Ibis. —Ed.

25. Mellemfolkeligt Samvirke, roughly "Cooperation between Peoples," founded in 1944, promotes "the political empowerment of the world's poor." Today, it is associated with the international ActionAid network. —Ed.

to prevent, or at least disrupt, the meeting, to train members in militant action, and to inspire others. One action that KAK members were involved in was a petrol bomb attack against the Bella Center where the congress was held.[26]

KUF and KAK members were also regularly sent to paint slogans like "Long Live PFLP" (*Leve PFLP*) and "Vietnam, Palestine—the same struggle" (*Vietnam Palæstina—samme kamp*) on bridges and commuter trains.

Today, we are convinced that for the KAK leadership the actions themselves were at least as important as their results. They wanted members of the organization to gain experience in illegal activities.

KUF/Anti-imperialistic Action Committee poster in protest against the World Bank congress in Copenhagen 1970: "The World Bank: This is where imperialism's most effective minions work in order to reinforce the exploitation of the oppressed and to increase the profits of the monopolists. We are on the side of the oppressed! Whose side are you on?"

---

26. The Bella Center is Scandinavia's largest exhibition and conference center; it opened in 1965. —Ed.

◆ *Tøj til Afrika*

With regard to the material support for liberation movements, KUF founded the organization Tøj til Afrika, TTA, in 1972. TTA mainly collected used clothes and sent them to refugee camps in Africa administered by liberation movements where they were distributed according to need. Many KUF and KAK members, as well as sympathizers, became involved in practical work through TTA: clothes needed to be collected, sorted, packaged, and shipped. Soon, the Copenhagen TTA activists were joined by local chapters in Odense, Løgstør, and Holbæk.

During the project's first seven years, the following amounts of clothes were sent:

1972	0.9 tons (to the MPLA in Angola)
1973	8.7 tons (to FRELIMO in Mozambique and to the PFLOAG in Oman)
1974	4.7 tons (to FRELIMO)
1975	13.3 tons (to the MPLA, to the PFLO in Oman, and to ZANU in Zimbabwe)
1976	9.1 tons (to ZANU)
1977	27.3 tons (to ZANU)
1978	ca. 70 tons (to ZANU)[27]

TTA also held flea markets in order to raise funds. The most successful flea markets brought about one hundred thousand crowns. Some of the money was used to ship the clothes, and the rest was donated to selected liberation movements.

◆ *The illegal work*

Both KAK's leadership and the rank and file were constantly looking for different ways to increase the organization's support for liberation movements. One of the possibilities was to acquire funds in illegal ways. None of us belonged to the KAK leadership when it was decided to pursue this path.

---

27. The organizations supported by TTA from 1979 to 1986 (when the project disbanded) were ZANU, SWAPO in Namibia, and the IRE in South Africa. —Ed.

Therefore, we can only take a qualified guess as to why this happened. The guess is based on discussions we have had throughout the years and on what Jan Weimann was told after he had joined the KAK leadership in 1975. There are strong indications for the illegal practice starting as an experiment. The KAK leadership wanted answers to the following questions:

- Was it possible to acquire significant economic means by illegal activities?
- Did the organization have members that could engage in such activities?
- Could the members engaged in these activities hide them from other KAK members as well as from people outside of the organization?
- Was it possible to engage in such activities without using excessive violence?
- Was it possible to engage in such activities without drawing the attention of the authorities?
- Could the activities be defended politically and morally?
- Would the members engaged in these activities answer these questions in the same way as the leadership?

It is important to remember that we did not go directly from collecting clothes to robbing cash-in-transit trucks. Members had partaken in violent demonstrations and direct actions before, such as the petrol bomb attack against the Bella Center. This made the step to robbery easier.

It did not take long before KAK's leadership considered the experiment successful. This, however, demanded some structural changes within the organization. In particular, security was tightened. As a result, socializing was not a big priority within KAK from 1972 to 1976. Contacts between members focused on the political work. One member close to the leadership was excluded because he was considered a security risk.

PØK claims that KAK's leadership already agreed to materially support the PFLP by illegal means when Gotfred Appel and Ulla Hauton met with PFLP representatives in Jordan in 1970. We do not believe that. When Gotfred and Ulla traveled to Jordan in 1970, the intention was to discuss politics. The discussions convinced them that the PFLP fulfilled KAK's criteria for support. PØK has no documentation for criminal activities being discussed, and the slow and experimental way in which KAK's criminal activities developed suggest that no such discussions took place.

Once the illegal practice was established, it had to be justified politically. The rationale was that as long as significant material support for Third World movements could be acquired without using excessive violence the means were legitimate. We will return to the political and moral aspects of the illegal practice in the section "Means and Ends."

This was, in short, the history behind KAK's criminal activities. The degree of violence we were ready to use was discussed before every action. This was a matter of great concern to us. We always tried to minimize the risk for the victims. For example, we put a lot of effort into making batons that would do as little harm as possible. At the same time, yes, we were willing to use batons, warning shots, and physical coercion. We justified this with the significant support that these means allowed us to provide for liberation movements. Regardless of what the exact original intentions of Gotfred and Ulla might have been, the main motivation for us to engage in these activities was always to support liberation movements as effectively as possible.

Our Relationship to the RAF, the PFLP, and Wadi Haddad

Let us be clear:

- ► We had no connections to illegal organizations in Western Europe, including the RAF in West Germany and the Red Brigades in Italy.
- ► We collaborated with the PFLP, not with Wadi Haddad.
- ► We were a self-governing and independent organization, not a PFLP cell.

We reject PØK's suggestion that KAK, and later M-KA, belonged to an international "terror network." PØK's claims are false; they are based on a small portion of facts and a big portion of imagination. He favors drama over documentation.

PØK suggests that we collaborated with the RAF. That is nonsense. Already in 1975, we published a critique of the RAF's theoretical and practical approach in *Kommunistisk Orientering*.[28] We never shared the RAF's analysis that West Germany was a fascist state with a democratic facade. Furthermore, the RAF wanted to support the struggle in the Third World by building an anti-imperialist front in Western Europe. We considered this utterly impossible. We never sent out a single communiqué to explain our actions precisely because of this. For us, there was no feasible revolutionary perspective in Western Europe. The change had to come from the Third World, and therefore the most important thing to do for Western anti-imperialists was to support Third World liberation movements materially. We have stated this over and over again in our articles, pamphlets, and books.[29]

The primary reason for us not having any contact to the RAF was therefore political. However, there was also a tactical reason. When we began collaborating with the PFLP, we also saw many other Europeans visiting them. We were not interested in meeting or even being recognized by them. In light of our illegal activities, any form of contact with the RAF or similar groups would have been a major security risk. Therefore we developed procedures with the PFLP that ensured us not having contact with other Europeans during our visits. We did not want an arrested RAF member mentioning a secret Danish group involved in robberies as a means to support Third World liberation movements. For the same reason, we avoided contact with Palestinian activists in Denmark. Only once, after we had lost contact with the PFLP during the breakup of KAK and the subsequent founding of M-KA, did we decide to get in touch with PFLP members living in Denmark. We instantly paid a price for this: the PFLP members were under surveillance by PET agents, who consequently also took an interest in us. We never repeated that mistake.

That the RAF and KAK/M-KA were very different organizations is also confirmed by the way they related to Palestinian organizations. We got in touch with the PFLP because we wanted to support them. The RAF got in touch with Fatah because they wanted them to provide military training and equipment.[30]

---

28. KAK, "Kritik af RAFs analyse og strategi" [Critique of RAF's Analysis and Strategy], *Kommunistisk Orientering* no. 5, 1975.

29. See, in particular, M-KA, *Imperialismen idag: Det ulige bytte og mulighederne for socialisme i en delt verden* (Copenhagen: Manifest, 1983); English edition: *Unequal Exchange and the Prospects of Socialism* (Copenhagen: Manifest, 1986).

30. Fatah is a left-leaning Palestinian political party founded in 1965. It is the

After the civil war in Jordan in 1970, a rift occurred between the PFLP and Wadi Haddad's Special Operations Group. The RAF was interested in collaborating with Wadi Haddad. We were not. Instead, we consciously distanced ourselves from him.

It is true that a number of meetings were held between the KAK leadership and Haddad. The purpose of these meetings was to gather information. What did his group stand for? Was its cause worth supporting? Did it seem feasible to collaborate with him? And, if so, did it seem possible to collaborate with him without putting our own activities at risk? Our security was important to us, because it was the basis on which we were able to do what we did.

We decided for various reasons not to collaborate with Haddad. The decision was unanimous among the KAK leadership. The reasons were the following:

- ► The most important one was that Haddad's actions had little to do with mobilizing the Palestinian people. Instead of creating popular resistance against the Israeli occupation, as for example the Intifada did, Haddad chose elitist actions, that is, actions that required a high level of training and sophisticated equipment. The effect was that the actions pacified rather than mobilized the Palestinian population because ordinary Palestinians could not partake in them. It was militant demonstrations and throwing rocks at Israeli soldiers that inspired widespread resistance.
- ► We were puzzled by the fact that Haddad had opened the first of our meetings by asking what we could do for him and by explaining what he could do for us. Practical collaboration seemed more important to him than common political ground. This went against our principles. We always discussed politics first.
- ► Haddad's operations simply became increasingly unsuccessful. When he had organized hijackings and similar high-profile actions as a PFLP member, his intention was to put the Palestinian question on the map. With this, he succeeded. After his split from the PFLP, however, all of his actions were fiascoes, both practically and politically.

strongest faction within the PLO. Its founder and longtime chairman was Yasser Arafat. —Ed.

> ► We thought that the PFLP had the right political analysis of the
> situation in Jordan after the so-called Black September of 1970: In
> the late 1960s, the Palestinian organizations in Jordan decided to
> be very open. They carried weapons in refugee camps and also on
> the streets of Amman. Jordan was also used as a base for opera-
> tions against the Israeli occupation in the West Bank. Palestinians
> comprised 60 percent of Jordan's population and King Hussein
> began to perceive them as a threat to his rule. In September 1970,
> he ordered a military attack on the refugee camps. The result was
> that the Palestinian organizations were forced to leave the coun-
> try and move to Lebanon. George Habash and Wadi Haddad had
> different answers to this. Haddad concluded that the resistance
> movement had to go underground since it was not strong enough
> for an open, and therefore vulnerable, presence in an Arab country.
> Habash concluded that the resistance movement had to stay above-
> ground and be visible, since this made popular support more likely.
> Besides, one needed to defend the refugee camps in Lebanon,
> especially in light of the right-wing Christian forces active in the
> country.

The reason why we decided to continue our collaboration with the PFLP under the leadership of George Habash was that it had the popular base that we
always saw as a precondition for supporting any movement. Once M-KA was
founded, the contact with Wadi Haddad and his group ceased completely.
Haddad died shortly after.

The RAF's connections to Haddad are well documented. Haddad was
behind the Landshut hijacking on October 13, 1977. The plane ended up
in Mogadishu, Somalia, where the hijackers demanded the release of imprisoned Palestinians and RAF members in exchange for the release of
the Landshut hostages. The operation ended in a defeat for Haddad when
a German antiterror corps stormed the plane and freed the crew and
passengers.

In the end, all that is true is that we knew someone who was collaborating
with the RAF. However, that's it, and it's a curious decision on PØK's part to
use eighty pages in his book to tell the story of the RAF. Don't get us wrong:
it is an interesting story and we understand that it increases the book's suspense value—it just has nothing to do with the Blekingegade Group.

PØK also claims that the KAK members traveling to meet with PFLP representatives did not get their passports stamped at airports in the Middle East. That is completely false. This only happened on the few occasions we met with Wadi Haddad in Baghdad. If PØK had bothered to look more carefully into the court documents, he would know that we used different passports. We needed them precisely because our passports *did* get stamped when we traveled to the Middle East. We usually claimed stamped passports lost so we got new ones. In fact, PØK could have simply contacted the Danish passport authorities to receive all the relevant information. But it certainly makes for a better story if he tells about young Danes secretly smuggled across Arab borders.

We Were a Self-Governing and Independent Organization

It is completely false to suggest that we were a "PFLP cell." This was never the way in which we related to the PFLP. In the context of a hierarchical organization, a "cell" receives orders from above. We always had full control over our activities. Our practice was determined by our own political analysis and our own strategic decisions. We have never had a meeting with the PFLP without discussing politics.

We did not primarily support the PFLP because it wished to establish a Palestinian nation state, but because the PFLP envisioned a socialist society in the Arab world and because it had an explicitly internationalist outlook. The PFLP trained many members of liberation movements in the Third World. The first FSLN guerrilla fighters, the so-called Nicaraguan Sandinistas, were trained in a PFLP camp in Lebanon. The Sandinistas went on to fight a successful liberation struggle and seized power in Nicaragua in 1979. Supporting the PFLP therefore had an important internationalist dimension for us, because it also meant supporting many other Third World liberation movements.

We were an independent group with our own political outlook. At times, this outlook differed from that of the PFLP. For example, we were skeptical of the PFLP developing close ties to the Soviet Union in the 1980s, and we criticized their commandos crossing the border from Lebanon for actions inside Israel, since the character of these actions was as elitist as Haddad's and often caused bloody reprisals by the Israeli state.

Historical Parallels: The Wollweber League

The Blekingegade Group as an organization involved in illegal and secret political work has been called unique in Danish history. But that is not true. There were others. If we want to find them, we have to go back to the time between the two world wars, when the so-called Wollweber League was active in the country.[31] The Wollweber League consisted of people who, after Hitler's rise to power in 1933, were convinced that everything had to be done to stop the Axis powers (Germany, Italy, and Japan), even if this included illegal actions on the territory of Denmark or other countries not ruled by fascist governments.[32] Denmark was a parliamentary democracy at the time, with the DKP being represented in parliament. Yet, this did not deter the Wollweber League members from bombing ships in Danish ports or smuggling weapons to Spain.

The perspective of the Wollweber League was international. Even if there was democracy in Denmark, international politics were not democratic. The dark clouds of fascism and Nazism threatened everyone. The Wollweber League members saw it as probable that the Axis powers would bring the world yet another gruesome war. The dilemma they were facing was similar

---

31. This history has been documented in Erik Nørgaard's *Krigen før krigen: Wollweber-organisationen og skibssabotagerne, fra den spanske borgerkrig til besættelsen af Danmark* [The War Before the War: The Wollweber Organization and the Sabotage of Shipping Traffic: From the Spanish Civil War to the Occupation of Denmark] (Lynge: Bogan, 1986) and *Krig og slutspil: Gestapo og dansk politi mod Kominterns "bombefolk", fra besættelsen af Danmark til idag* [War and Endgame: Gestapo and Danish Police against the "Comintern bombers": From the Occupation of Denmark to the Present] (ibid.), volumes 3 and 4 of a four-volume history of the Comintern.

32. The Wollweber League was named after its founder, the German communist Ernst Wollweber, who, as a young sailor in the Imperial German navy, was involved in the Wilhelmshaven Revolt of 1918, which led to the German Revolution and the end of the Kaiserreich. After the Nazis seized power in Germany in 1933, Wollweber fled to Copenhagen, where he set up an "organization against fascism and in support of the Soviet Union," i.e., the so-called Wollweber League. The Wollweber League was responsible for more than twenty acts of sabotage—mainly in Northern Europe—against ships serving fascist powers. Wollweber was arrested in Sweden in 1940 and deported to the Soviet Union in 1944. After the war, he was a high-ranking member of the East German SED. —Ed.

to ours: Was it justifiable to use illegal means to damage Danish property and to even endanger innocent people when you had the option to work legally within the democratic framework? As shown by their actions, their answer was yes. Here are three examples:

1. On September 3, 1935, Kaj Gejl used a petrol bomb to damage the American ship *United States* in the port of Copenhagen. After three failed attempts, he succeeded with the fourth. The *United States* was going to be sold to Italy. Mussolini wanted it for the transport of troops to Abyssinia, where Italy was engaged in a brutal war of conquest.

2. On May 22, 1938, Alberti Hansen and Kaj Thandrup Christensen blew up two Spanish trawlers in the Frederikshavn shipyard. The trawlers had been ordered by the Spanish government before the civil war, but, given the course of the war, it had to be assumed that they would end up in the hands of Franco. Franco would have most likely equipped them with cannons and used them to attack the naval shipments of weapons to the Republican troops. He had already done so with a trawler that had fallen into his hands earlier.

3. This concerns not a single event but a solidarity campaign: during most of the Spanish civil war, Richard Jensen chartered ships—the so-called *krudtbåde*, or "powder boats"—to transport weapons and ammunition to the Republican forces. These ships were manned by Danish seamen who volunteered to take the (significant) risk to sail to Spain. Almost one thousand Danish mariners served on these boats.

Just like the Blekingegade Group, the Wollweber League had no desire to make it known that it stood behind these actions. In order for their fight against the fascists to continue, they had to remain invisible.

Another parallel between the Wollweber League and us was the massive disapproval both groups met. Parts of the left called us "Maoists," "lunatics," "terrorists," "anti-Semites," and so forth. When the Wollweber League blew up the Spanish trawlers in Frederikshavn, the left reacted no differently. In an article published after the event in the DKP's journal *Arbejderbladet* [Workers' Journal], the party's central committee had the following advice

for its readers: "Watch out for provocateurs consisting of Trotskyists, inform-
ers, Gestapo agents, and Nazis! ... Beware of these elements and their king-
pins, who we will soon expose."[33]

However, there was also an important difference between the Wollweber
League and us. The Wollweber League had close ties to the Comintern and
was controlled by the Communist Party of the Soviet Union. We have always
been completely independent. It is true that some of our actions were recommended to us by others—but it was always us who decided whether we
wanted to do them or not. We were in charge, also on the occasions we "bor-
rowed" people from other organizations: they always acted under the leadership of the Blekingegade Group.

Above: Vridsløselille State Prison yard in the early 1940s, when several Wollweber League
members were imprisoned there, half a century before the Blekingegade Group members.
Right: The DKP reacts to a Wollweber League bombing in 1938: "From the Central
Committee to the chapters and members: Beware of Provocateurs!"

---

33. Quoted from Erik Nørgaard, *Krigen før krigen: Wollweber-organisationen og
skibssabotagerne, fra den spanske borgerkrig til besættelsen af Danmark.*

PARTIET

Fra Centralkomiteen til Afdelinger og Medlemmer:

Vær paa Vagt mod Provokatører!

Kammerater!

Den udenlandske og indenlandske Reaktion og dens Forbundsfæller foruroliges ved vort Partis Fremgang, ved vor stigende Indflydelse paa Folkets offentlige Mening og vor Kamp for en Indenrigspolitik i Landets og Folkets Interesse.

Derfor søger man af al Magt at finde forfatningsmæssige og ikke forfatningsmæssige Paaskud til Angreb paa vort Parti og spejder endog efter Muligheder til Overgreb i Form af Forbud o. l.

I selve vort Partis Politik eller Virksomhed finder man imidlertid ikke de forønskede Paaskud, hvorfor man bestræber sig paa *dels stedvis* at forvrænge Partiets Politik, *dels* at paalyve os andre Maal og Hensigter end vi har *og endelig* ved Provokationer, som Tilfældet „Frederikshavn" viser det at skade vor Anseelse og skaffe „Begrundelse" til Indskriden mod os.

Den forbryderiske Hensigt blev øjensynlig ikke naaet med Provokationen i Frederikshavn. Saa meget mere ivrigt har visse lyssky Krese, hvis „Arbejdskraft" bestaar af Trotskister, Stikkere, Gestapoagenter og Nazister, i den senere Tid bestræbt sig for at trænge ind i Partiets Rækker eller organisere Terrorhandlinger og Provokationer. Saadanne Forsøg gøres i særlig Grad i København, men forsøges ogsaa i Partiet eller blandt dets Sympatiserende i visse Provinsbyer.

Centralkomiteen erklærer kategorisk, at ethvert Forsøg paa at vinde Partiorganisationer eller Medlemmer for Handlinger, som strider mod Landspartikonferencens Aand eller Beslutninger stammer fra forbryderiske, partifjendtlige Krese, der handler i Fascisters og ligesindedes Interesse. Vi advarer disse Elementer og deres Bagmænd, som vi skal vide at afsløre for Offentligheden. Vi opfordrer hele Partiet og Ungdomsforbundet og alle vore Medlemmer til størst mulig Agtpaagivenhed, til politisk Aarvaagenhed og til øjeblikkelig at søge Samarbejde med Partiledelsen, hvor de kommer ud for de af Klassefjenden betalte Marodører og deres Virksomhed.

D. K. P.s CENTRAL-KOMITE
POLIT-UDVALGET.

Manifest–Kommunistisk Arbejdsgruppe

In describing the successor to KAK, that is, Manifest–Kommunistisk Arbejdsgruppe, M-KA, we want to focus on three aspects:

- the end of authoritarian leadership;
- the theory of unequal exchange, which was more nuanced than KAK's analysis;
- M-KA's continuation of both legal and illegal support for Third World liberation movements.

The KAK Split

In 1977, personal animosities and power struggles within KAK escalated. Initially, Gotfred Appel and Ulla Hauton were KAK's undisputed leaders, surrounded by enthusiastic but unschooled militants in their early twenties. By the end of the 1970s, however, many members had a decade of political experience behind them, they had traveled, organized solidarity projects, and so on. They had matured and developed their own perspectives. Some of them were bothered by KAK's internal discipline that didn't allow for theoretical improvements. Neither the transformation of imperialism nor events like the oil crisis led to adjustments of KAK's political foundations. Ideas for projects were never put into practice, because members were not used to doing things without receiving orders. Furthermore, there were personal conflicts. Ulla felt disrespected by male members. Gender discrimination was without doubt a problem within KAK, and this was the time when the Redstockings movement was strong, also in Denmark.[34] Eventually, it all came to a head when female members, with the approval of the leadership, demanded that male comrades undergo "criticism and self-criticism" sessions. Men who refused to participate were threatened with expulsion. This was serious, as membership in KAK was central to KAK members' lives. Politically, there was nowhere else to go either. Not many organizations on the left prioritized practical support for liberation movements. KAK members were proud of their organization.

---

34. *Rødstrømpebevægelsen* is the Danish term for the international feminist-socialist Redstockings movement, founded in New York City in 1969. —Ed.

The criticism and self-criticism sessions lasted through the winter of 1977–1978 and effectively put a halt to all other activities. Female members demanded the expulsion of several men. Friendships and relationships were put to the test. Eventually, it became obvious to several members, both men and women, that things had gotten out of hand. Upon their initiative, a few meetings for the rank and file were organized. The leadership was not invited. The first of these meetings took place on May 4, 1978. About thirty members gathered in a house, where a few of them lived communally. The meeting's agenda was to end the anti-gender discrimination campaign and to analyze how things could have gone so wrong. What were the problems within our organization that had allowed this to happen? A few days later, Ulla and Gotfred were called to a meeting in order to present their views. Ulla was furious and insisted on the campaign continuing. In the end, Gotfred came to the meeting alone and suggested suspending all KAK activities for half a year; then, the leadership would present a proper analysis of the events. The majority of the members rejected this proposal; they wanted to analyze the reasons for the anti-gender discrimination campaign and the course it had taken them. In the end, the members expelled Gotfred and Ulla from KAK after a vote.

During the following summer, KAK's political orientation, practice, and structure were discussed at numerous membership meetings. It became obvious that there was disagreement about how to deal with the mistakes that had been made and how to move on. Long papers with evaluations, future plans, theoretical reflections, and practical suggestions were written and discussed. It looked as if the debates would go on forever. The three authors of this article and some others grew increasingly frustrated with the practical part of our work lying idle. We felt that we had a responsibility both toward the Tøj til Afrika activists and to the liberation movements we collaborated with. They were all wondering what was happening. Our group was willing to continue the political evaluation of KAK's history and the development of future perspectives, but we also wanted to get back to practical work. In August 1978, we presented our thoughts for everyone and announced the founding of a new organization. This effectively split the former KAK into three groups:

▸ Gotfred Appel and Ulla Hauton, who had refused to accept their expulsion, continued to work under the name KAK. In *Kommunistisk Orientering* they declared that they had expelled the rest of the membership. They returned to being loyal to Beijing and followed the line of the CPC without reservation. The liberation movements they now supported were the ones that China supported. Chinese foreign policy at the time was built on a division of the world in three parts, whereby the two competing imperialist powers—the USA and the Soviet Union—controlled the rest. China saw the Soviet Union as the more aggressive power of the two, against which the rest of the world had to be defended. This meant that Third World nations and Western countries had a common interest in fighting the Soviet Union. KAK uncritically adopted this "Three Worlds Theory." Among others, they supported Pol Pot in Cambodia.

▸ Some former KAK members founded the *Marxistisk Arbejdsgruppe*, MAG. They intended to continue with the analysis of KAK's past mistakes, while trying to develop a new form of organization and solidarity work. MAG was only short-lived. It folded in 1980.

▸ The three of us and a handful of other former KAK members prepared a new organization. Everything that was related to the illegal practice was moved to a safe location. We reestablished contact with the liberation movements we had collaborated with and explained the new situation. We rented office space and established a print shop. The majority of the Tøj til Afrika activists in Copenhagen and the TTA chapter in Odense decided to work with us. Later, another TTA chapter was established in Århus.

The Foundation of Manifest–Kommunistisk Arbejdsgruppe (M-KA)
On September 3, 1978, Manifest–Kommunistisk Arbejdsgruppe was officially founded. In the beginning it consisted of only seven members, including Holger Jensen and the three of us. In October, the first issue of our journal *Manifest* appeared. The first article, "Kommunistisk Arbejdsgruppe dannet" [Communist Working Group Founded] outlined our perspectives and

intentions.[35] In certain ways, we felt like we were KAK's heirs, but we also wanted to develop our own analysis and improve our practice.

M-KA's organizational goal was different from KAK's. Even if Gotfred Appel considered revolutionary development in Denmark to be highly improbable, he intended to build an organization that had the resources, the knowledge, and the discipline to act once a revolutionary situation in the country would occur. In the end, his support for Third World liberation movements had a clear Danish perspective:[36] KAK was to be ready for the day the revolution returned to Western Europe.

35. M-KA, "Kommunistisk Arbejdsgruppe dannet" [Communist Working Group founded], *Manifest* no. 1, October 1978.

36. See, for example, the pamphlet *Det kommer en dag—Imperialisme og Arbejderklasse* (Copenhagen: Futura, 1971), published in English as *There Will Come a Day: Imperialism and the Working Class* (ibid.).

For M-KA, supporting liberation movements was a revolutionary end in itself. Any possible revolution in Denmark was too far away and too abstract to even consider. Rather, we saw three things as being crucial: to develop political analysis and theory; to spread our analysis and theory; and to continue with the illegal and legal practice. We wanted to provide material support for liberation movements as an organization with a solid independent analysis. The Danish perspective moved further and further into the background and gave way to a thoroughly global perspective. One could say that M-KA was a reflection of "globalization" before the term was invented. Our logo combined a globe with a five-pointed star.

Establishing a new organization set an enormous amount of energy free. We had been in the doldrums for almost a year. The authority of Gotfred Appel and KAK's internal discipline had been hindering independent initiatives and developments even longer. Now there were new possibilities. It was time to act again.

M-KA's Structure

M-KA was a small, but hard-working group. People were either "full-time activists" on unemployment or they dedicated all of their free time to the organization. Some people left, others joined. The membership was always around twelve to fifteen people. Because of the illegal work, new members were only fully included after a year, once we had gotten to know them well. There was a bigger circle of sympathizers and volunteers who helped with the legal solidarity work. Our journal *Manifest* had about two hundred paying subscribers.

The way M-KA was organized marked a rupture with the centralism and closedness of KAK. We had a democratically elected leadership and, all in all, a horizontal structure. We wanted to form an organization able to develop its politics by way of internal as well as external discussion. Holger was a driving force in the early days of M-KA, but solely because of his dedication—he had no formal leadership role. His death in 1980 was a hard blow to us. However, the following years proved that M-KA had become strong and grounded enough to continue its work nonetheless. Administrative, theoretical, legal, and illegal tasks were assigned on the basis of mutual agreement.

This gave the organization stability and made it effective.

It is clear that the illegal practice set limits as to how open M-KA could be. Only those involved in the illegal practice knew the details. But the decision about which liberation movements to support was taken by the entire organization. We had also established an offset print shop and a publishing house in the northwest of Copenhagen. There we printed journals of liberation movements, information material for Tøj til Afrika, and, eventually, a series of pamphlets and books.[37] The expenses were paid for by member contributions, which depended on the individuals' means. In some cases, those were quite high.

Holger Jensen, 1979.

37. See the website http://www.snylterstaten.dk for a list of Manifest publications. —Ed.

The Development of M-KA's Politics

To advance political theory was important for M-KA. We arranged study groups together with Tøj til Afrika. We set up a small library at our space in northwest Copenhagen. This was before the Internet age, so we subscribed to the BBC World Service, which had daily news cables coming from the Middle East, Southern Africa, and other regions. This allowed us to keep ourselves updated on the developments in regions in which we supported liberation movements.

We were convinced that in order to develop an effective practice we needed to study economic and political relations and to have a concrete analysis of where and how to get involved in people's struggles. Our practice was always informed by strategic and tactical reflections that we dedicated much time to. An important factor was the discussions we had with liberation movements and the experiences we shared with them. We developed our political perspectives together.

We also resumed our travels. M-KA members went to Zimbabwe, Mozambique, South Africa, Botswana, the Philippines, and different countries in the Middle East. The entire M-KA membership visited the PFLP in Lebanon in 1981, both to discuss politics and to give members who had never been to Palestinian refugee camps an opportunity to see them.

From Lenin to Unequal Exchange

Gotfred was a Leninist. If there was a theoretical problem, his answer was, "Well, let's see what Lenin had to say." All answers could be found in Lenin's *Collected Works*—one just had to open the right one of the forty volumes. KAK's analysis of imperialism was based on Lenin's 1916 text "Imperialism, the Highest Stage of Capitalism."

In the mid-1970s, KAK tried to update Lenin's analysis in the spirit of Varga and Mendelsohn's book *New Data*.[38] For years we studied capital export to the Third World and profit rates. We studied the development of transnational corporations and the extraction of raw materials. Eventually,

---

38. E. Varga and L. Mendelsohn (eds.), *New Data for V.I. Lenin's 'Imperialism, the Highest Stage of Capitalism'* (Moscow: Foreign Languages Publishing House, 1939).

Arghiri Emmanuel and Torkil Lauescn, 1983.

we had to conclude that Lenin's analysis of imperialism was no longer ap-plicable. Foreign direct investments and profits could no longer explain the rising gap between the rich countries and the poor. However, KAK was not able to draw the necessary conclusions and revise its theory.

M-KA did not have that problem. We were able to react to the changes that the analysis of imperialism had gone through in the 1970s. The Egyptian economist and historian Samir Amin had spoken of the rich countries form-ing the "center" and the poor and dependent countries the "periphery" of a global economic system that led to Third World poverty and underdevel-opment. The American sociologist Immanuel Wallerstein had described the historical development of the world system and the division of poor and rich countries from the fifteenth century to the present. And Arghiri Emmanuel had presented the theory of "unequal exchange": rather than capital export and superprofits, unequal trade was the reason for the world being divid-ed into rich and poor countries. Unequal exchange happens when goods are produced in Third World countries where wages are low and sold in rich countries where wages are high. Unequal exchange can, in short, be described as the result of different pay for the same kind of work.[39] What impressed us particularly with Emmanuel's approach was how scientific it was. His analysis was a direct continuation of Marx's *Capital*. It had the same basis: a thorough examination of theories and analyses of foreign trade from the nineteenth-century classical economists to this day. Each argument was examined carefully.

We first contacted Emmanuel in 1974, but the connection became much closer after KAK's split. Following the foundation of M-KA, we went to visit him several times. He also kept in touch after our imprisonment, and contact only ceased when he died in 2001. When we worked on our book *Imperialismen idag*, he read the manuscript and was kind enough to provide a preface. It included the following paragraphs:

> Often in meetings, academic or other, where I was to put the case for my theses on unequal exchange and on the international exploitation which was its outcome, sincere left-wing militants, somewhat at sea, asked the same question in different forms. If this is the case, if the proletariat no longer exists in our industrialized countries, if all, or almost all wage-earners, white collars and blue collars together, have become a labour aristocracy by definition producing less value than their wages allow them to appropriate and thus becoming the objective allies of imperialism, which brings them the supplement, what, then, becomes of the political action of revolutionary marxists? To whom, to which class, to which strata of society can they therefore address themselves? ...
>
> This is the question to which the members of the *Kommunistisk Arbejdskreds* have replied in this book. One must, they say, quite

---

39. See, in particular, Samir Amin, *Unequal Development: An Essay on the Social Formations of Peripheral Capitalism* (New York/London: Monthly Review Press, 1977) [French original: *L'impérialisme et le développement inégal* (Paris: Editions de Minuit, 1976)], Immanuel Wallerstein, *The Modern World System* (New York: Academic Press, 1974), and Arghiri Emmanuel, *Unequal Exchange: A Study of the Imperialism of Trade* (New York: Monthly Review Press, 1972) [French original: *L'échange inégal: Essai sur les antagonismes dans les rapports économiques internationaux* (Paris: François Maspero, 1969)].

simply, put oneself at the service of the classes which have an interest in overthrowing imperialism, "... no matter where they are geographically." This is clearer and more distinct than anything I have been able to mumble in answer here and there to my various questioners. ...

Now, as a result of some historical changes which Marx could not forecast, classes are no longer distributed "geographically" today, according to the classical intranational model. The proletariat, the true party to the cause of the socialist revolution, has practically disappeared in the affluent countries of the centre. It continues to exist in the periphery. ...

The structure of this book reflects the progress of their praxis, as I have been able to witness it through personal contacts I have had with them. Firstly to know the world, then to transform it. But ... to know the world as it is today and not as it was in Marx's time and nevertheless to do this by using the marxist method.[40]

In *Imperialismen idag* we tried to give a realistic estimation of unequal exchange. Using trade figures and wage statistics we calculated that in 1977 about 350 billion U.S. dollars were transferred from the Third World to the rich (OECD) countries.[11]

Emmanuel withdrew from the academic world in the late 1980s. He died in 2001 at the age of 90. Since then, different people have continued to study unequal exchange. If one set the exchange balance to zero in 1865, then calculations of trade, wages, and purchasing power show that unequal exchange led to a transfer of value equivalent to 1,750 billion U.S. dollars from poor to rich countries in 1995, which equaled 6.6 percent of the gross world product. The three biggest losers of unequal exchange in 1995 were China, Mexico, and Indonesia. The three biggest winners were the U.S., Japan, and

---

40. Arghiri Emmanuel, "Preface," quoted from the English edition of *Imperialismen idag*: M-KA, *English Unequal Exchange and the Prospects of Socialism* (Copenhagen: Manifest, 1986), 9–15.

41. The Organisation for Economic Co-operation and Development (OECD) was founded in 1961 by industrialized nations committed to a market economy. In 2012, it consisted of 34 member states. —Ed.

Germany. Today, unequal exchange leads to a transfer of value equivalent to more than 2,000 billion U.S. dollars per year. This amount is many times higher than foreign aid, private credits, and corporate investments going to Third World countries combined.

Other Studies

Some of the results of the studies we did in M-KA were published in our journal *Manifest* and in pamphlets and books.[42] We examined the historical origin of the world's division into rich and poor countries; we looked at why some former colonies—in South America—remained poor, while other former colonies—in North America—developed and became rich; we studied crisis theory and capitalism's ability to adapt and transform; we studied the Soviet Union's development in the 1980s; we looked at U.S. military strategy in the Third World after the Vietnam War.

We were constantly searching for new information and discussed our perspectives both with political allies and academics. In the mid-1980s, we were involved in starting a political journal, *Liberation*, which was distributed in Tanzania and Uganda. In short, we find it difficult to accept PØK's portrayal of M-KA as a rigid and dogmatic organization.

Solidarity Work

M-KA proceeded with the legal solidarity work that KAK had started. Tøj til Afrika continued to send tons of clothes, shoes, and tents to camps hosting refugees from Zimbabwe, Mozambique, Namibia, and Angola. We visited these camps to make sure that all the deliveries arrived. Together with Ulandsklunserne,[43] we arranged monthly flea markets. The earnings went to political refugees from South Africa or to the PFLO in the Arab Gulf. We also spread information about the liberation movements we supported.

---

42. See the website http://www.snylterstaten.dk for a list of Manifest publications. —Ed.

43. See p. 38 n. 23. —Ed.

In 1983, we published a book about the conflict in the Western Sahara.[44] In 1985, we were involved in starting the Western Sahara Committee (Vestsaharakomité), which supported refugees from the region. We were also involved in the Namibia Alliance (Namibiaforeningen), the Philippines Committee (Filipinerkomité), and the El Salvador solidarity campaign.

In 1987, we opened Café Liberation in the Islands Brygge district, near the center of Copenhagen. The café was exclusively run on voluntary labor. All earnings went to liberation movements.

We had four criteria for deciding which movements to support:

- a socialist perspective
- broad popular support
- strategic significance for the struggle against imperialism
- a tactical consideration: we wanted our limited means to be used in ways that made a difference. This is why we often supported movements during the earliest phase of their struggle, when they did not yet receive much other support.

Let us name one example: In the early 1980s we supported the Black Consciousness Movement, BCM, in South Africa. The BCM largely consisted of students and youths in poor townships around Johannesburg. We printed a journal related to the movement, *Islandwana Revolutionary Effort*, as well as flyers and posters. We sent the material to Botswana, from where it was smuggled into South Africa. We also supported a pig farm and a bottle store in Botswana, which were managed by political refugees from South Africa and functioned as a base for actions on South African territory.

This is just one example that proves that our support work was more diverse—in terms of both the form it took and the people it reached—than what PØK makes his readers believe.

The reason for continuing the illegal practice was first and foremost that it allowed us to provide much bigger quantities of material support than our legal activities.

---

44. M-KA, *Konflikten om Vestsahara: Polisarios kamp for et uafhængigt land* [The Western Saharan Conflict: Polisario's Struggle for an Independent Country] (Copenhagen: Manifest, 1983).

Liberation

No. I   **July/Aug 1985**   **12 Shs**

Contents:

Editor: Karrim Essack

Published and printed by Manifest Press, Landskronagade 2, 2100 Copenhagen, Denmark. Responsible under

Danish law: K. Hansen   All correspondance to the editor: P.O. Box 937, Dar es Salaam, Tanzania

First issue of *Liberation*, July/August 1985.

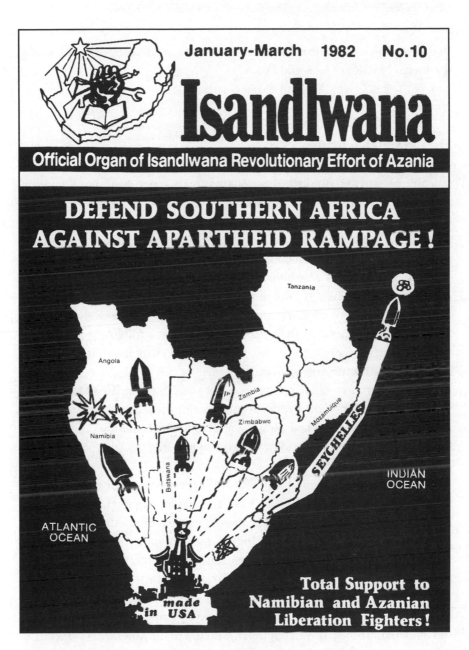

IRE journal, printed by M-KA.

THE CRIMINAL ACTIVITIES AND THE TRIAL

In this section we want to correct some of the wrong perceptions concerning the illegal practice of KAK and M-KA.

The Criminal Activities

KAK was already involved in illegal activities in the late 1960s. This included painting slogans in support of the Vietnamese and Palestinian liberation struggles on bridges and commuter trains, actions directed against the sale of Israeli goods in Brugsen supermarkets as well as against the involvement of Denmark's ØK company in teak logging in Thailand, and militant protests against the *Green Berets* screening in 1969 as well as against the World Bank congress in 1970. KAK also helped a group of Indonesian communists who were stranded in Eastern Europe after Suharto's coup and the massacres of Communist Party members in 1967. They wanted to secretly return to Indonesia to help reestablish the Communist Party. KAK arranged for them to travel from Hungary to Denmark, provided them with fake papers, and arranged for the return journey to Indonesia.

Of course it was a big step to go from these activities to acquiring money for liberation movements by illegal means. But these activities functioned as a kind of bridge. They had shown which of the KAK members were ready for illegal action and they had trained these members in careful and secret planning.

KAK wanted to provide the liberation movements with more support than it had been able to so far. This was the main motivation for the first robberies. In the beginning, they were mainly experiments. After they proved successful, they became an increasingly important part of KAK's practice.

PØK and other authors seem very excited about the idea of KAK members receiving training in Middle Eastern training camps. In their books, they return to this idea again and again. The problem is that no KAK members ever received training in Middle Eastern training camps. Yes, we have visited the PFLP many times. However, guerrilla tactics in the Middle East and criminal activities in Denmark have very little in common. In order to do what we did—in terms of planning, dealing with the security forces, and living a double life—one needed very specific knowledge about the conditions in Denmark. The PFLP couldn't provide that. We had to learn all this ourselves.

As we have already mentioned, the motives of the KAK leadership for the illegal practice were not necessarily the same as those of the individuals involved. We believe that the leadership had two major motives: to provide financial support for the liberation movements and to train KAK members in illegal activities. For us—none of whom was part of the leadership at that time—there was only one motive, and that was to support the liberation movements as effectively as possible. That was the reason for agreeing to participate in these actions when we were asked to.

We always discussed options other than robberies. We thought about making money through investments—but no one in KAK (or M-KA, in later years) knew anything about investments. We had one member who knew about IT, but his knowledge did not allow for great moneymaking schemes. Jan Weimann has been called an IT expert in the press, but his former colleagues probably only got a good laugh out of that. The only time that IT knowledge was relevant for any of our actions was during the forgery of postal money orders in 1976 that gave us 1.4 million Danish crowns.

The conclusions we drew from the robberies we conducted from 1974 to 1976 were the following:

- Detailed and careful planning was necessary in order to remain in control. In particular, an escape route was needed that made chases impossible or, at least, very difficult.
- You could never expect rational reactions from the victims. For example, you could never count on threatening someone into handing you the money, you had to take the money yourself.
- Moments of surprise and fear were important in order to minimize resistance and therefore the use of violence.

We never thought about the psychological trauma we could cause. At least partly, this can be explained by the fact that psychological trauma was not discussed much at the time. Obviously, this has changed. There is no doubt that we underestimated the psychological effects that our actions had on others. Whether we would have acted differently if we had had a better understanding we don't know, but we are certainly not proud of the psychological damage we have caused.

With every action we reached for a larger take. In a sense, this also increased the likelihood of something going wrong—both for the victims and for us. We tried to remain true to our principles, but we clearly made some wrong decisions along the way.

The organization that got the biggest support from us was the PFLP. The situation of the Palestinian people was very difficult. We also got to know PFLP members very well. We always acted based on our conscience, but the desperate situation of the Palestinians made us shift our limits. A number of events in the Middle East were very important for our practice: King Hussein's attack on the Palestinian refugee camps in Jordan in 1970; the Lebanese civil war; the massacre at the Palestinian Tel Al Za'atar refugee camp in 1976, in which about six thousand Palestinians were killed; Israel's heavy-handed repression of the Intifada; and the Israeli invasion of Lebanon in 1982.

The Rausing Kidnapping Plan

In particular the massacres in the refugee camps Sabra and Shatila[45] made M-KA members believe that it was worth taking higher risks for both ourselves and the victims of our crimes. There was a strong sense that the PFLP now needed all the support it could get.

At first, the kidnapping of a German millionaire, a co-owner of the Würth company, was planned. The tip had come from the PFLP. We abandoned the plan because we felt that the victim was not well chosen. We were unsure about whether we could get a big enough ransom—or any ransom at all. Since we never came close to executing the plan, our emotional and moral limits were not tested.

Then we turned to a new plan, this time focusing on the Rausing family in Sweden. Jörn Rausing, a heir to the rich Tetra Pak company, was living in

---

45. In September 1982, at least eight hundred Palestinians were killed during a three-day period by Christian Phalangist militias in the Beirut refugee camps of Sabra and Shatila; the Israeli army, which controlled the area at the time, was accused of not interfering and even of providing logistical support. —Ed.

Lund, in the south of the country, not far from Copenhagen. We always had bad feelings about the plan. But time and time again, we overcame our reservations. We ground our teeth, thought of the situation the Palestinians were in, and continued. This is not meant as an excuse, it is a simple description of what happened.

The closer we got to the date set for the kidnapping, the more difficult it became to push our reservations aside. The date was postponed several times. The smallest obstacle was turned into a big deal—in hindsight, we simply couldn't see the action through. There were a variety of reasons for this, whose importance probably differed from individual to individual.

First, there was the possibility of things going wrong; the plan was very complex and there were a number of risk factors.

Second, there was always the possibility that no ransom would be paid. We were quite certain that the Rausing family could and would meet our demands. But we could not be a hundred percent sure, which was bothering us. Besides, the whole thing went against our principle of taking money instead of threatening others into giving it to us.

Third, we couldn't do this with only a limited degree of violence. Our plan was to drug Jörn Rausing and to take him to a hiding place in Norway. We tested the methods we wanted to use (both the drugs and the means of transport) on ourselves to get a better understanding of their consequences. We discussed this issue endlessly, never reaching any satisfying conclusions.

Fourth, we felt empathy with the victim. We had gotten to know Jörn Rausing quite well during the months we had been observing him. Had he been an unpleasant fellow, it would have probably been easier to execute the plan. However, he appeared to be a pretty average and quite likeable young man.

Fifth, there was a strong emotional dimension. In the end, we were simply appalled by the idea of kidnapping someone, and this feeling only became stronger with time. This was probably the most important reason.

In hindsight, it was idiotic to even consider this kind of crime. It would have been way too harsh on the victim and it went beyond our capacities. When the time came, we simply weren't able to do it. Therefore, once the plan had been abandoned, we all concluded that we would never consider anything like this again. We decided that we should return to what we knew instead, which was robbery.

We thought that we could get away with the most spectacular coups, as long as the planning was right. However, it is difficult to be active for almost twenty years without making small mistakes. A single small mistake might not get you caught, but the mistakes add up and make you vulnerable. In retrospect, it wasn't the actual robberies that made PET suspicious of us. It was the mistakes we had made in our communication with the PFLP and an increasing carelessness regarding security.

Living a double life had become normal for us. We got a lot of satisfaction out of being "good craftsmen" able to provide organizations with the money they needed. At the same time, the life we led included a lot of stress, bad conscience, and many sleepless nights. We will return to this in the last section of this article.

The Weapons in Blekingegade

Many weapons were stored at the Blekingegade apartment. Most of them came from burglaries at a Danish Army weapons depot in the water tower of Jægersborg and a Swedish Army weapons depot in Flen. This is an aspect of our activity that we regret for several reasons.

For our operations, we needed small weapons for the purpose of intimidation during robberies. So why did we amass hand grenades, land mines, antitank missiles, and explosives? As we explained at our trial, the weapons were meant to go to liberation movements. Our main plan was to smuggle them into Israel or the occupied West Bank. After the Israeli invasion of Lebanon and the massacres in the refugee camps of Sabra and Shatila, the PFLP expressed a strong need for weapons. We wanted to help.

To get weapons and to store them was not a big problem. The problem was to come up with a good plan to get them to Israel and the Palestinian territories. Unfortunately, we had not made such a plan before we got the weapons. Once we had them, it took us a long time to come up with ideas. In the end, all we were able to do was to set up a secret weapons cache in France where we were able to deposit at least some of the weapons and explosives for PFLP members to collect.

Before that, we had planned to smuggle weapons into Israel disguised as surfers. We found a car ferry that could take us from Greece to Israel. We also looked at different types of cars. Our choice fell on a Ford Grenada. It seemed most suitable for carrying concealed weapons. We also cut up a surfboard, put two antitank missiles inside, and glued the board back together. It was done so professionally that the police were still wondering what the surfboard was doing in the Blekingegade apartment after they had turned everything upside down several times. Eventually, Torkil asked his lawyer to tell the police about the contents. He was afraid that the missiles might explode if the board was handled carelessly.

Obviously, we were set on doing the trip ourselves. It was clearly easier for Europeans to smuggle weapons into Israel than for Palestinians. But we had our doubts. What if we were discovered? None of us wanted to spend time in an Israeli prison. So, we shelved the plan and it didn't take long before we stopped considering it altogether. Instead, we contemplated getting rid of the weapons. But this wasn't so easy either. We certainly didn't want them to be discovered by anybody else. And how do you defuse an antitank missile?

PØK suggests that the weapons were meant for terrorist activities in Europe. That is incorrect. Just as incorrect as PØK's claims about our contacts with the RAF, the Red Brigades, and Carlos the Jackal, or about our alleged collaboration with Wadi Haddad. But, once again, it adds to PØK's tale if he can turn us into pawns of an "international terrorist network."

Needless to say, it wasn't smart to get all those weapons without a plan of how to transport them to their intended destination. It also meant that we ourselves gave rise to rumors about being involved in "civil war" and "terrorism" in Europe. However, as with all other aspects of our practice, the objective was simply to support Third World liberation movements. Not only did we reject military actions in Denmark and the rest of Western Europe morally and politically, but being involved in them could have also proven disastrous for our illegal practice, since it might have turned us into a prime target of the security forces.

In the end, the material support we were able to provide consisted of money, technical equipment, medicine, and clothes. We had the intention of providing weapons as well, but we failed to do so. That's the reason why the weapons were found in Blekingegade. They caused us many logistical problems and exposed the Blekingegade tenants to an entirely unnecessary risk in the case of fire. This is something we regret.

The "Mild Spy Paragraph," §108

Paragraph 108 of the Danish penal code became relevant during our trial because of the "Z-file" (Z for Zionism), often referred to as the "Jew file" in the press.

In 1981, the PFLP asked us to help identify people working for the Israeli intelligence service in Denmark. It was known that the Mossad used England and Denmark as informal headquarters of its European activities. In those countries, they were well received by the national intelligence services and guaranteed good working conditions. In France and Italy, for example, the relationship with the national intelligence services was much more complicated. This has also been confirmed by the former Mossad agent Victor Ostrovsky.[46] We ourselves had first-hand knowledge of Mossad agents trying to infiltrate Palestinian circles in Denmark.

The PFLP told us that they became increasingly suspicious about some of the many "left-wing tourists" from around the world coming to visit them in the Middle East. One example concerned the underground base in the Beirut refugee camp of Burj el-Barajineh. Visitors had inquired about the thickness of the walls. During the invasion of Lebanon in June 1982, the base was destroyed by so-called bunker busters. The PFLP felt that if they had a list of people possibly working for the Israelis, it would be easier to identify spies.

At first, we were hesitant. This kind of work was time-consuming and if we indeed got close to a Mossad agent it would put our own practice at risk. Yet, particularly in light of the Israeli invasion of Lebanon, we wanted to help. We decided to add another person to the illegal practice in order to handle the extra work that was required. This person was Bo Weimann, who, as a trained librarian, had the qualifications needed for the job. The Z-file became his main project.

We started with the assumption that anyone recruited as a Mossad agent in Denmark would have probably voiced pro-Israeli views at some point in the past. So we were looking for pro-Israeli (Zionist) sympathizers who suddenly stopped voicing their opinions in public.

---

46. Victor Ostrovsky and Claire Hoy, *By Way of Deception: The Making and Unmaking of a Mossad Officer* (Scottsdale: Wilshire Press, 1990); on Denmark, see pages 231–33 and 241.

The Z-file originally consisted of two parts. The first one listed companies, organizations, and periodicals that were pro-Israeli. The second one listed individuals who had voiced pro-Israeli opinions. The only concrete results of this work concerned the Wejra case.[47] We also identified one individual as a possible Mossad agent. In an attempt to produce more concrete results, we added a third part to the Z-file, listing everyone who had signed a petition in support of Israel in 1973.[48] The idea was to compare this list to the other two in order to find possible overlaps. A significant number of the individuals listed were—unsurprisingly—Jewish. That is why some journalists wrongly referred to the file as a "Jew file."

We want to be very clear about one thing: We *are not* and *have never been* anti-Semites. We reject the Zionist project, whose objective has always been to create a purely Jewish state. The Palestinian people were displaced and their homelands occupied by Israel in two wars, in 1948–1949 and in 1967. We demand that the United Nations live up to their own resolutions guaranteeing the Palestinian people the right to a sovereign nation state. The United Nations have never enforced these resolutions. The Palestinian people have a legitimate right to resist the Israeli occupation, and we are on their side.

The Death of a Policeman during the Købmagergade Robbery

During our trial, two of us gave statements about the Købmagergade robbery and the shot that caused the death of a policeman.[49] We explained that the intention behind the shot was to puncture the police vehicle's tires in order to prevent a chase. The prosecutors conceded that the shot was fired from the hip and unsighted. This was also confirmed by witness statements and the forensic evidence whose conclusion was that the policeman was hit by a stray pellet in the eye. The other pellets riddled the display window of a shoe store.

---

47. Wejra was a Danish weapons manufacturer that was accused in the 1980s of secret relations with Israel involving financial irregularities, illegal arms trade, and espionage. The company closed in 1990. —Ed.

48. The petition expressed support for Israel during the Yom Kippur War. —Ed.

49. Torkil Lauesen and Carsten Nielsen. See also "Solidarity Is Something You Can Hold in Your Hands" in this volume. —Ed.

Bent Otken, the presiding judge, drew the following conclusion: "According to all the information we have, including the rapid development of events in Købmagergade, it cannot be assumed that the robbers had collectively agreed to fire at possible pursuers with the intent to kill."[50] Therefore, Otken recommended that the jury not sentence us for intentional murder and we were acquitted on this count.

During the trial, it had not been possible to prove—or even make it appear probable—that this was a case of premeditated murder. If this had been the case, all of us could have been found guilty of murder. This was the conviction that the police were seeking.

We never reckoned that firing shots would be necessary during the Købmagergade robbery. We thought that the alarm from the cash-in-transit truck would go to the post office first, then from there to the police. According to our calculations, the probability of police arriving at the scene within less than two minutes was minimal. Unfortunately, we were wrong. During the trial, we came to understand that the alarm had gone directly from the truck to the police. Had we known this beforehand, our plan would have looked different. It was always mandatory for us to avoid direct confrontations with the security forces.

What was our plan in case a police patrol did arrive at the scene? In fact, two of them arrived. We met the first one in Løvstræde, right after turning out of the post office yard. We managed to pass it before two shots were fired at our van. One shattered the back window and got stuck in the driver's seat. The second patrol car was waiting for us on Købmagergade. We pulled into the opposite direction and acted according to our plan, which was to stop and fire a warning shot against any vehicle trying to follow us, whether it was a police car, a post office truck, or a taxi. We carried a shotgun with us because it made a lot of noise. It was also loaded with big pellets that could puncture the tires of any possible pursuer. Unfortunately, one of those pellets hit the policeman.

Of course it implies a risk to bring a weapon to a robbery and to fire a warning shot. But none of us ever intended to take someone's life. We deeply regret that it came to that. We cannot change what has happened, no matter how much we would want to.

---

50. From the stenographic transcript.

Entrance to the post office yard where the Købmagergade robbery took place on November 3, 1988. (photo: Rebecka Söderberg)

PET and Us

We were under observation by PET for almost twenty years. We do not believe that this has ever happened without us being aware of it. Otherwise, it would have been impossible to gather at secret apartments several times a week for all this time without ever disclosing them.

The observations began in 1970, when Holger attracted attention in connection with the demonstrations against the World Bank congress. He enjoyed switching roles and began following the agents.

We developed a routine for how to behave when we noticed that we were observed. We acted as normally as possible, not letting anybody know that we were aware of the observation. Anything else would have seemed suspicious. We also developed methods to ensure that we were not observed when it would have compromised us.

PET agents were always easy to recognize. They were in their thirties and about six feet tall, they had nice clothes and usually were in good shape. There were always two people in a car. The cars were unassuming middle-class models in modest colors. Usually, three to four cars were working in shifts. The time patterns were very steady. We could often count on the observation ending on Friday at 4:00 PM and recommencing on Monday morning. Sometimes, things were done more professionally, but even then

75

it hardly ever took more than a few minutes before you knew that someone was following you.

Niels and Holger were observed when they came home from the U.S. in 1979. It was basically revealed to them during a stopover in London. They were searched and questioned about their journey. When they asked for a reason for the interference, they were told, "We know very well what kind you are."

Our homes were also searched. Sometimes, the agents didn't return things to their proper place, or they were forced to leave in a hurry. We were convinced that our phones were tapped, and always used them carefully. When Torkil applied for a job at the Foreign Ministry, he was told that he could not be cleared. We knew that PET had an eye on us.

Our analysis was that PET knew about our contacts with the liberation movements, especially the PFLP, and that this was what made us interesting. They probably also knew that we were involved in illegal activities, but they didn't know the details. When we were arrested in 1989, it became obvious that PET's knowledge was limited. They arrested Peter Døllner who hadn't been active in the group for many years, while they apparently didn't know about the members who had joined later.

MORALITY AND POLITICS

The third and final section of the article addresses the connections between morality and politics, including the use of violence in a political context.

Violence has always been a central part of politics. This is an uncomfortable truth. Since World War II, there have been more than a hundred armed conflicts in the Third World causing the death of more than twenty million people. It is easy in contemporary Denmark to take a moral stand and reject violence as a political means, even if in reality most people are willing to use it, not least government officials. The boundaries between legitimate peacekeeping missions and criminal violence and terrorism depend largely on one's political orientation. It is all about politics.

On the following pages we want to investigate both the claim that the ends justify the means and the claim that the ends never justify the means. We want to provide examples of the dilemmas you inevitably encounter as a political militant. We want to discuss the use of violence as a political means. And, finally, we want to shed some light on the relationship between liberation struggles and terrorism.

Do the Ends Justify the Means?

Among other things, PØK's books about the Blekingegade Group caused a fiery debate about the group's morals. With PØK's "voice" as the main reference point,[51] most commentators agreed that the Blekingegade Group's approach was "cynical." We were portrayed as supporters of hijackings and of people using criminal means to achieve their goals. It was suggested that we blindly followed the motto of "the end justifying the means." This is a statement often ascribed to Niccolò Machiavelli, author of *The Prince*, a little book written in the early sixteenth century. *The Prince* consists of numerous guidelines for how to govern. However, it is far from the first text to discuss the relationship between ends and means. In the tragedy *Electra*, the Greek dramatist Sophocles asked in 400 BC whether "the end excuses any evil," while, in 10 BC, the Roman poet Ovid concluded in his lyrical collection *Heroides* that "the result justifies the deed."

Balancing ends and means requires concrete reflections on what you find important and justified. If someone pursues ends that you do not consider important, it is easy to morally discredit the means. The accusation of someone following the principle of "the end justifying the means" comes easily. It is always convenient if you can accuse people you disagree with of immorality. On March 4, 2007, *Politiken*, one of Denmark's biggest dailies, wrote, "Overall, the 'voice' admits that the end justified the means; that it was okay to do anything as long as it served the cause." The Blekingegade Group was portrayed as a group of amoral villains that had turned against the apparent social consensus that the ends never justify the means.

---

51. In Peter Øvig Knudsen's books about the Blekingegade Group, one of his sources is an anonymous former M-KA member, referred to as the "voice." After the book's publication, it was officially revealed that the voice belonged to Bo Weimann. —Ed.

Let us, for a moment, consider political reality rather than noble rhetoric. Is there really a consensus on the end never justifying the means? Here are three examples regarding the war in Iraq ...[52]

> On December 5, 1996, shortly after being appointed U.S. secretary of state, Madeleine Albright was interviewed by Lesley Stahl for the TV program 60 *Minutes*:

>> *Stahl: "We have heard that a half million children have died. I mean, that's more children than died in Hiroshima. And—and you know, is the price worth it?"*

>> *Albright: "I think this is a very hard choice, but the price— we think the price is worth it."*

> On January 1, 2004, the Danish prime minister Anders Fogh-Rasmussen declared in his New Year's television address to the nation: "I am certain that the liberation of the Iraqi people was and is worth all costs."
> On February 20, 2005, Tøger Seidenfaden, the editor of *Politiken*, commented: "Seen with Western eyes, the noble end—democracy in the Middle East—justifies the harsh means." This statement was made two years after the invasion, when the enormous number of victims was already known.

Apparently, when it comes to the war in Iraq, the consensus that the ends never justify the means is not valid.

If the motto of the end justifying the means implies that you can use any means you want (without any consideration for the consequences for others) in order to achieve any end you have decided to pursue, then the Blekingegade Group has never followed such a motto. At the same time, we have never followed the motto that the end *never* justifies the means either. After all, there is a third option—which, in fact, is much more realistic than the other two: not *all* ends justify *all* means, but, depending on

---

52. The examples are taken from Jørgen Bonde Jensen, *Politiken og krigspolitik-ken—et læserbrev* [Politics and War Politics: A Letter to the Editor] (Copenhagen: Babette, 2007).

the circumstances, *some* ends justify *some* means. This was the position that guided our actions. It is a position, of course, that implies challenges. One has to consider and balance three factors: ends, means, and circumstances. It is not always easy to draw the right conclusions.

We do not believe that Albright, Fogh, or Seidenfaden would argue that all means are justified once you have decided to pursue a certain goal (even if they obviously go a pretty long way: half a million dead children, seven hundred thousand casualties, and four million displaced Iraqis). The point, however, is that political actors have to be very clear about both their ends and their means. This requires a political discussion. Morality plays an important role in this discussion, but a reference to moral principles alone is not enough. In the eighteenth century, Immanuel Kant argued that the end alone can never justify the means, and that means need to be justifiable in and by themselves. This is an important reminder that the means we employ need to be carefully examined. But Kant's argument does not rid us of the responsibility to go through a political discussion first.

Most people find violence acceptable if the end is important enough and the situation urgent. For example, few people in Denmark would—politically or morally—question the use of violence in the context of the Danish resistance movement against the Nazis. Presumably, they would hold the same opinion even if the Nazis had won the war. By itself, the Danish resistance movement was not strong enough to defeat the Nazis. They were but a small wheel in the fight against them. Yet, the end of weakening Nazi Germany was enough to justify the use of violence. The resistance fighters sabotaged factories and railways in order to interfere with the production and delivery of goods important to the German war industry. Suspected collaborators were assassinated. But this does not mean that all means were acceptable. In recent years, some actions have also been criticized—for example, certain assassinations were based on weak evidence. Still, the overall opinion remains that under the given circumstances, the use of violence was justified.

It is hard to say where exactly the legitimate use of violence begins. In the case of the Danish resistance movement, the lines were drawn by the individual resistance groups and the individual resistance fighters. It was them who had to live with the decisions for the rest of their lives. This is the simple core question of each political dilemma: *What do I do?*

We also chose to be a small wheel in a big struggle. In this case, it was the global struggle against oppression and exploitation in colonies, settler states, and Third World dictatorships. We also have to live with this decision for the rest of our lives.

Machiavelli's Use of "The End Justifying the Means"

Machiavelli's book *The Prince* was published in 1532. It is a manual for the art of governing. It includes Machiavelli's famous (and infamous) justifications of violence as a means to secure power. For example, he states that "a prince wishing to keep his state is very often forced to do evil."[53] Essentially, the book is an honest description of how power functions, regardless of all ideological and moral considerations. One can read *The Prince* in various ways. To read it as a cynical manual for how to gain and defend power, is one option. Machiavelli himself, however, suggests another reading: "It being my intention to write a thing which shall be useful to him who apprehends it, it appears to me more appropriate to follow up the real truth of the matter than the imagination of it."[54]

Machiavelli was one of the Renaissance's first secular thinkers. He wrote about separating religion (the dominant form of morality at the time) and politics. He refused to analyze political realities on the basis of religious dogma. He was, in contrast to many of his contemporaries, a realist, and he could not help but notice how far removed the theological idealizations were from the real and harsh world of politics. It is also important to remember the historical and political context in which *The Prince* was written. Machiavelli's intention was not to aid royals in their exercise of power; it was to unite Italy.

Italy reached national independence in the fifteenth century based on a balance of power between five states: Naples, the Papal State, Florence, Milan, and Venice. Governance relied on strict rules, implemented by a tight-knit system of diplomatic representation. But from 1494 onward, Italian unity was attacked by France and Spain. Naples and Milan lost their independence and the other three states were under constant threat. In

---

53. Niccolò Machiavelli, *The Prince*, translated by W.K. Marriott, http://www.gutenberg.org/files/1232/1232-h/1232-h.htm.

54. Ibid.

other words, the advice on ends and means that Machiavelli presented in *The Prince* was not based on general principles, but on a concrete historical situation, namely a nation being besieged. The same can hardly be argued in the case of the USA in 1996 (Albright) or of Denmark in 2004 (Fogh) and 2005 (Seidenfaden). The existence of neither state was threatened when the above statements were made. Arguably, in 1970, the situation was different for the Palestinians.

The 1970 PFLP Hijackings

When, in September 1970, PFLP commandos hijacked three civilian planes and ordered the pilots to fly to the Jordanian desert, the Palestinian nation was in a desperate situation. The U.S. secretary of state, William Rogers, had outlined a plan for the Middle East known as the Rogers Plan. The PFLP and most other Palestinian organizations as well as political observers considered the plan a blueprint for quelling the Palestinian resistance and eradicating any hope for a Palestinian state. This perception was strengthened by the U.S.-approved attacks of the Jordanian military on the Palestinian refugee camps, which had commenced a few months earlier. The PFLP hijackings have to be understood against this background. They were if you allow us this figure of speech—an attempt to pull the emergency break in a situation that threatened the Palestinian struggle as a whole. The feeling was that something needed to be done to prevent the Rogers Plan from being implemented. It must also be noted that the hijackings ended with the airplanes being blown up, while all of the hostages remained unharmed.

It was not the first time that the PFLP had responded to attacks by taking hostages. When the Jordanian air force bombed Palestinian refugee camps for five days, from June 7 to 11, 1970, PFLP commandos occupied two of Amman's main hotels and took the American, West German, and British guests hostage, demanding an end to the bombardments. At 5:00 AM on June 12, 1970, the PFLP's general secretary, George Habash, gave a speech before the hostages at the Jordan Intercontinental Hotel. What follows is an excerpt:

> Ladies and gentlemen! I feel that it is my duty to explain to you
> why we did what we did. Of course, from a liberal point of view
> of thinking, I feel sorry for what happened, and I am sorry that

81

we caused you some trouble during the last two or three days. But leaving this aside, I hope that you will understand, or at least try to understand, why we did what we did. Maybe it will be difficult for you to understand our point of view. People living different circumstances think on different lines. They cannot think in the same manner and we, the Palestinian people, and the conditions we have been living for a good number of years, all these conditions have modeled our way of thinking. We cannot help it. You can understand our way of thinking when you know a very basic fact. We, the Palestinians for twenty-two years, for the last twenty-two years, have been living in camps and tents. We were driven out of our country, our houses, our homes and our lands, driven out like sheep and left here in refugee camps in very inhumane conditions. For twenty-two years our people have been waiting in order to restore their rights but nothing happened. Three years ago circumstances became favorable so that our people could carry arms to defend their cause and start to fight to restore their rights, to go back to their country and liberate their country. After twenty-two years of injustice, inhumanity, living in camps with nobody caring for us, we feel that we have the very full right to protect our revolution. We have all the right to protect our revolution. Our code of morals is our revolution. What saves our revolution, what helps our revolution, what protects our revolution is right, is very right and very honourable and very noble and very beautiful, because our revolution means justice, means having back our homes, having back our country, which is a very just and noble aim. You have to take this point into consideration. If you want to be, in one way or another, cooperative with us, try to understand our point of view.[55]

Habash's words take us back to the original question of this chapter: "Does the end justify the means?" Did the twenty-two years of displacement and

---

55. Habash's speech was copied from the PFLP's website (http://www.pflp.ps) a few years ago, where it is no longer accessible.

miserable living conditions in refugee camps—now exposed to bombardments—justify the occupation of hotels and the hijacking of airplanes? At this point, the question becomes concrete. It is no longer about abstract philosophical arguments, but about making a concrete political decision. Did these particular ends—the halting of bombardments of refugee camps and the creation of an independent Palestinian homeland—justify these particular means used under these particular circumstances? We thought they did. We tried to understand the PFLP's perspective. But that doesn't mean that there were no limits to the means that were justified, also for the PFLP. In both cases—the occupation of the hotels and the hijackings of the planes—the hostages remained unharmed.

The English philosopher Ted Honderich has approached this question differently, but he reaches the same conclusion: an occupied people has the right to resist and, if necessary, to use violence. He refers to the "principle of humanity" as a way to distinguish between a legitimate and an illegitimate use of violence. For him, the Palestinian situation is an example for what he considers a legitimate use of violence:

> I have drawn a parallel between the resistance against the apartheid regime in South Africa and the resistance against the occupation of the Palestinian territories. When a people are oppressed and their homelands occupied, you cannot deny them the right to use violent means of resistance. ... One lives a poor life when one cannot expect to live a long and healthy life, when one enjoys neither freedom nor civil rights, has neither respect nor self-respect, and possesses no possibility to create relationships with others and partake in cultural development. A politics that seeks to establish a good life corresponds to the principle of humanity. The Palestinians' terrorist acts can be justified because they are directed against a power that denies them a good life. That's why their struggle is legitimate, while, for example, Osama bin Laden's is not.[56]

---

56. "Nogle gange kan terror retfærdiggøres" [Sometimes Terror Can Be Justified], Interview with Ted Honderich by Mads Qvortrup, *Information*, December 27–28, 2008, 14–15.

With respect to our approach, Ted Honderich looks at one of the factors we need to consider when deciding how to act politically: the justification of ends. He does not address the justification of means.

Struggling for Liberation Is Not Terrorism

The international actions of the PFLP and other Palestinian organizations from 1968 to 1972 made the entire world aware of the Palestinian situation. In the late 1960s, the Palestinians felt that no Western politicians or journalists even bothered to listen when they tried to tell them about their plight. As an old Palestinian told us, they felt like the "donkeys of the world."

When KUF members put up posters in Copenhagen in 1969 in order to raise awareness about the situation of the Palestinians, the only statements of sympathy were unwished for because they came from the political right. To express support for the Palestinian struggle was considered anti-Jewish. Regarding the PLO's international actions, for example, Noah Lucas has written that although this "earned it little sympathy in the world, it nevertheless succeeded in establishing the image of its cause as the quest of a victimized people for national self-determination, rather than a neglected refugee problem as it had hitherto been widely regarded."[57]

The Palestinian demand for an independent state was practically ignored by the West, despite resolutions passed by the UN as early as 1947 (Resolution 181: Partition Plan for Palestine) and 1948 (Resolution 194: Right of Return for Refugees), both expressing a commitment to an independent Palestinian homeland. It is worth noting that the Western countries themselves had voted for these resolutions.

We found it both necessary and justified to support the Palestinian liberation struggle, especially in the context of commitments to and responsibility for a just global order. Either UN resolutions are binding for all, or one accepts the doctrine of "might makes right." We considered the situation of the Palestinians so hopeless and miserable that "dirty" methods, such as hijacking planes, would at least give them a chance to be heard. We did not see the PFLP's struggle as terrorism. The PFLP fought for a democratic and

---

57. Noah Lucas, *The Modern History of Israel* (London: Weidenfeld & Nicolson, 1974), 437.

nonreligious state. Palestinians lived under the occupation of violent security forces.

The PFLP's political leader was Abu Ali Mustafa. He worked openly in the West Bank, but was killed when an Israeli Apache helicopter fired two missiles into his office in Ramallah on August 27, 2001. The offices of Palestinian leaders in Ramallah are protected by the Oslo agreement, which Israel co-drafted and signed. Yet, the Israeli government decided to execute Abu Ali Mustafa without judicial process. According to the Israeli human rights organization B'Tselem, Israel has killed 232 Palestinians since the year 2000 in so-called "targeted killings," that is, in assassinations executed by the state with no legal foundation. These assassinations have also caused the death of 154 civilians. This has not led to any noteworthy international reactions.[58] Israel does not act like a constitutional state. In the occupied territories, there is no rule of democracy, only the rule of the fist.

The PFLP responded to the assassination of Abu Ali Mustafa on October 17, 2001, with the assassination of the Israeli minister of tourism, Re'havam Ze'evi. Ze'evi had probably been involved in the decision to kill Abu Ali. He was the leader of the National Union, an alliance of ultra-right nationalist parties, which, after the terror attack on the U.S. on September 11, 2001, had advocated ethnic cleansing by demanding that all Palestinians should be forced out of Israel and the occupied territories. The killing of Ze'evi was the reason for the PFLP being added to the list of terrorist organizations by the U.S. and the EU. So, when the PFLP uses violence against a state—even if it is an occupying power—this is condemned and called terrorism. When that same state uses violence against the people living under its occupation, it is called retaliation and self-defense. Sometimes, when Israel acts in a particularly brutal manner, there is some international criticism. But the only organizations that end up on the list of terrorist organizations are those formed by the people living under occupation.

A simple count of the victims that the conflict in the region has caused shows that the Israeli state has killed about five times as many people as Palestinian militants. According to B'Tselem, 4,789 Palestinians were killed by Israeli security forces or by Israeli civilians between September 29, 2000, and April 30, 2008. During the same period, 1,053 Israelis were killed by Palestinians. If one looks at the numbers for minors, there were eight times

---

58. Quoted from *Berlinske Tidende*, December 6, 2008.

as many Palestinian victims as Israeli ones: 938 vs. 123. According to the same source, the majority of Palestinians killed were not selected targets but random civilians.[59] The international community might "regret" the violence of the Israeli state, while the violence of the Palestinians is condemned and criminalized. No one ever calls the support of the Israeli state criminal.

Violence as a Political Means

Politicians love to talk about democracy. They hate to talk about violence. This stands in complete contrast to both historical experience and political reality. Politicians all over the world implement and use growing apparatuses of violence. Also the Danish government uses violence increasingly in its foreign policy. The "peace dividend" promised after the fall of the Berlin Wall never came.

We have no romantic relationship to violence. We have seen the civil war in Lebanon with our own eyes. We have seen torched villages in Rhodesia. On television, we have seen bombs dropped from B-52s over Vietnamese cities, and we have seen children burned by napalm running from the jungle. However, we have no romantic relationship to nonviolence either. We did support the armed liberation struggles in many countries.[60]

It is not surprising that anti-colonial and anti-imperialist struggles turned violent. The violence of European colonialism and imperialism was extreme. Two lesser known examples are the following: the German colonists exterminated almost the entire population of South-West Africa (today's Namibia) in 1904,[61] while in 1902, after taking over the colonial administration from the Spanish, the U.S. sent 125,000 troops to the Philippines to quell the liberation movement—the war cost the lives of half a million people.

The colonial attitude was summarized by the former British prime minister Lord Salisbury in his 1898 speech at Albert Hall: "You may roughly divide

---

59. See http://www.btselem.org/english/statistics/Casualties.asp.

60. See also Torkil Lauesen, *Det globale oprør* [The Global Uprising] (Copenhagen: Autonomt forlag, 1994). On armed struggle and peace, see pages 117–31.

61. Sven Lindqvist, *Udryd de sataner* (Copenhagen: Gyldendal, 1992), 168; English edition: *Exterminate All the Brutes* (New York: The New Press, 1997).

the nations of the world as the living and the dying ... the living nations will gradually encroach on the territory of the dying ..."[62]

The imperialism of the twentieth century has been equally brutal. The U.S. killed one million people during the war in Vietnam. France's attempt to save the French settler regime in Algeria also cost one million people their lives.

It was against the backdrop of the Algerian struggle that Frantz Fanon, who was active in the Algerian liberation movement, wrote the book *The Wretched of the Earth*, in which he reflects both on his own situation and on the situation of Third World nations in general. He concludes that the people of the Third World—held down by violence, exploitation, and oppression—must rise and gain self-consciousness. He argued that liberation from the colonial system and independence could be achieved by violent resistance coordinated and led by liberation movements. In his preface to *The Wretched of the Earth*, Jean-Paul Sartre wrote:

> Try to understand this at any rate: if violence began this very evening and if exploitation and oppression had never existed on the earth, perhaps the slogans of nonviolence might end the quarrel. But if the whole regime, even your nonviolent ideas, are conditioned by a thousand-year-old oppression, your passivity serves only to place you in the ranks of the oppressors.[63]

Our perspective was that systems of violence, often with the involvement of the U.S., stood in the way of democratic liberation and socialism. Take, for example, the CIA's role in the coup against the democratically elected government of Salvador Allende in Chile in 1973, or the CIA's endless meddling in the affairs of the countries of Central America. There was no hope for liberation without armed struggle in the Portuguese colonies of Mozambique and Angola, the racist regimes of Rhodesia and Southern Africa, or the right-wing dictatorships of Latin America.

---

62. Lord Salisbury, "Speech at Albert Hall," May 4, 1898, quoted from Andrew Roberts, "Salisbury, The Empire Builder Who Never Was," *History Today* 49, no. 10, http://www.historytoday.com/andrew-roberts/salisbury-empire-builder-who-never-was.

63. Jean-Paul Sartre, preface to *The Wretched of the Earth* (1961), quoted from http://www.marxists.org.

Most liberation movements had originally been founded as legal political movements. South Africa's ANC is one example. It advocated a nonviolent struggle until the late 1950s. Only after the Sharpeville massacre in 1960[64] and the subsequent criminalization of the ANC did the organization turn to armed struggle.

In 1970, there was a wave of rebellions spanning the globe from Vietnam to Mexico and from South Africa to the U.S. We felt that this was the beginning of a revolutionary process we wanted to see grow. We were far from the only ones supporting armed struggle. In the early 1970s, the belief in armed struggle was much more commonplace within the left than it is today. This was also expressed in the publishing world. The back cover of the Danish edition of *The Wretched of the Earth* cites Klaus Rifbjerg's review of the book in *Politiken*: "One of the most important texts—perhaps *the* most important— about the struggle in colonized countries is now available in Danish; it reveals an almost poetic anger and, at the same time, a compelling objectivity."

In 1971, the renowned Danish publishing house Gyldendal released the anthology *Den palæstinensiske befrielseskamp* [The Palestinian Liberation Struggle] edited by Jens Nauntofte. It included interviews with Leila Khaled on hijackings and with George Habash on international politics. The book's tone is very positive. It clearly speaks of a "liberation movement." Militants who are called "terrorists" today, are referred to as *fedayeens* in the book, the Arab word for "partisans" or "those who sacrifice themselves."

The sympathies of the left for the liberation struggles were met by criticism from the right. The boundary ran, unsurprisingly, right through the Social Democrats. Prime minister J.O. Krag and the minister for foreign affairs, Hækkerup, supported the U.S. war in Vietnam. Only when Anker Jørgensen criticized the 1972 Christmas carpet bombing of Hanoi did the party begin to change its position.[65] The U.S. dropped 7.6 million tons of bombs over Indochina. That is three times the amount of all bombs dropped by the Allies combined during World War II.

---

64. On March 21, 1960, sixty-nine people were killed when the South African police opened fire during a protest outside the police station of the township of Sharpeville, south of Johannesburg. —Ed.

65. Jens Otto Krag, Per Hækkerup, and Anker Jørgensen were prominent members of Denmark's Social Democrats (*Socialdemokraterne*). —Ed.

The bourgeois camp, represented by the *Berlinske Tidende* and *Jyllandsposten* newspapers, were certainly no principled opponents of the use of violence as a political means. Both defended the war of the U.S. in Vietnam until the very end. *Jyllandsposten* also expressed sympathies for Pinochet's coup against Allende in Chile and deemed South Africa's black population not ready for democracy. Erhard Jakobsen, the founder of *Centrum-Demokraterne*, was a staunch supporter of the apartheid regime and considered ANC members to be terrorists.[66] The ANC's leader, of course, was Nelson Mandela—the celebration of Mandela as a great statesman is a more recent phenomenon.

What was our personal situation like in the late 1960s and early 1970s? We witnessed a global uprising on the one hand, and lived privileged lives in a Western country on the other. Our conclusion was that we had to act. We felt that there existed incredible injustice in the world and we wanted to contribute to a profound political and economic change. We also felt that we were in a position that allowed us to act, and that it would have been inexcusable if we didn't.

We find it difficult to share the perspective of the "voice" in PØK's book when it states that "one can never compare different forms of suffering." To begin with, the quest for a better and more just world does not begin with a cost-benefit analysis. It begins with a simple statement: "Enough!" Reflections about what you can achieve, and at what price, come later. Secondly, if you want to act politically, you cannot escape such reflections. That was true for us, and it has been true for anyone who has ever been involved in political struggles. Why bother with global economic justice, social welfare, or health care if you do not want to alleviate suffering? How can you fight an occupying power, resist oppression, and rise up, if you're not affected by certain forms of suffering in a particular way? We all are affected by certain forms of suffering in a particular way in our everyday lives. We care more about people who are close to us than about people we don't know or who we count among our enemies. That is human. Everything else enters the realm of divinity.

---

66. *Centrum-Demokraterne* [Center Democrats] was a Danish center-right party that split off from the Social Democrats in 1973; the party dissolved in 2008. —Ed.

We do not think that we gave ourselves "a moral free pass," as PØK's "voice" suggests. There were always lines we wouldn't cross in our activities. Morality was always important, and we had innumerable discussions about the moral implications of our practice. This became very clear in relation to the Rausing kidnapping. All of us had problems with the idea. At the same time, we had been strongly affected by the Israeli invasion of Lebanon, the thousands of people killed, and the massacres of Sabra and Shatila. The struggle of the Palestinians was our struggle. They were our friends. We felt close to them and therefore shifted our moral boundaries—for a while. But that didn't mean that anyone was issued a "moral free pass." The plan, and the related anguish, took a hard toll on us all. A "moral free pass" would have meant to do nothing.

Global and National Contexts

Of course it was problematic to use violence in Denmark. But we did not see our practice as limited to the Danish context, we saw it in relation to a global struggle. We acted in a world that was divided between rich and poor countries; a world without global democracy in which the principle of "might makes right" determined international relations. Anti-imperialist movements with a democratic agenda and no backing by an armed liberation movement didn't stand a chance against an imperialism armed to the teeth and ruthless in the execution of its power. From our perspective, transferring value from the rich countries to the poor, specifically if received by liberation movements, was justified.

Here is a concrete example: In 1947, the UN accepted—with Denmark's vote—a partition plan for Palestine with the goal of establishing both an Israeli and a Palestinian state. Years went by and neither Denmark nor the UN security council did anything to enforce this resolution. While the Israelis had their state, the Palestinians were languishing in refugee camps. So what do you do as a democratic Danish citizen? Do you play by the democratic rules of your country or do you promote democratic rights internationally? What shall a democratic internationalist do when rich and powerful democracies lose all sight of democratic values in their foreign policies, and when this leads to people being robbed of the right to establish their own independent state? Does this make it justified to support their cause with illegal means? Those were the questions we were facing.

In this world of inequality, we lived and acted in a country in which there was no desire for revolutionary change. That's why we did not send out communiqués explaining our actions, in contrast to organizations like the RAF, the Red Brigades, and others we have been associated with. In the Danish context, our activities were simply criminal. That was also the reason why we never felt that the legal system was treating us unjustly and why we never saw ourselves as political prisoners. In the context of the Danish state and legal system, we were criminals, pure and simple. We had answered the questions we were facing in a particular way, and we had to accept the consequences—even if the motivations for our criminal activities were rooted in an analysis of the global political system.

Of course there are problematic implications to acting undemocratically in a democratic country in order to promote democracy in an undemocratic world. Then again, there are also problematic implications for democratic countries to send their armies out into the world without any democratic principles. The war in Iraq is a case in point. This fundamental contradiction—between national democratic systems and undemocratic international relations—has not lost its significance in the age of globalization.

CONCLUSION

There have been many stories circulating about the Blekingegade Group for the past twenty years. They aren't going away. Quite the contrary. The media always returns to the subject and law enforcement officers and politicians are happy to jump on the bandwagon. They have a particular motive: a hatred for the left of the 1970s. Apparent "investigations" are actually part of a political battle. People like Peter Øvig Knudsen and Jørn Moos also have personal motives of course. They want to sell books, work as "advisors" for film, TV, and theater, appear on talk shows, and give talks across the country. On the back cover of PØK's two-volume history of the Blekingegade Group it says: "This is a documentation. The text is not the result of the author's imagination; it is based on innumerable written and oral sources." This is a truth with modifications.

We understand that the story of the Blekingegade Group is a good story. But it is not as spectacular and meaningful as some try to make it to be. The "Blekingegade Group" is on its way to becoming a label exploited by the media industry. It is turning into a money-making machine. But who owns the copyright to the story? We know that capitalism likes to lay claim on everything. However, this doesn't mean that we have to play along.

In this article, we wanted to present our experiences and reflections in a condensed form. It is meant neither as an apology nor as a manifesto. It is, however, an attempt at telling our history in a political context. Instead of focusing on crime and drama, we would like to see a more nuanced debate about politics, ends, and means.

We also wanted to pass on the experiences of twenty years of work with KAK and M-KA, which can hopefully contribute to forming new political strategies.

The story of the Blekingegade Group is a story about political action as a reaction to the political action of others. It provides an example of how to connect national and international politics. It is a story of anger at injustice and a will to change the world. It is a story about doing something, since doing nothing was not an option for us. It is a story about political analysis and about reflections on what is true and what is not.

Global exploitation and inequality were the main causes of our political actions. As we know, global exploitation and inequality still exist. But so do the movements trying to end suffering and oppression. The struggle continues.

Unequal exchange illustration, M-KA, ca. 1982.

Solidarity Is Something
You Can Hold in Your Hands

Interview with Torkil Lauesen and Jan Weimann

The interview was conducted by Gabriel Kuhn in Copenhagen in the spring of 2013. All footnotes in this interview by the editor.

KAK and the Parasite State Theory

How did you first get involved with KAK?

Jan: I was interested in politics because of my family. Both my mother and my father were in the DKP. Together with other students from my high school, including Holger Jensen, I started going to demonstrations against the Vietnam War. Holger was the first who had connections to KAK. There was also a student who was very interested in political theory. He showed me a series of articles that KAK had published under the name "To linjer" in *Kommunistisk Orientering*.[1] Reading those articles was a revelation to me. They described convincingly why the class struggle had no perspective in Denmark and why it was necessary to support revolutionary movements in the Third World instead. As a consequence, I went from moral opposition to the war to theoretical study and activism. KAK's ties to China, which were still intact at the time, weren't that important to me. I was mainly attracted

---

1. "To linjer" [Two Lines] 1–6 were published as inserts in *Kommunistisk Orientering* from no. 18, 1968, to no. 2, 1969.

by the parasite state theory, and in 1968, I joined the Anti-imperialist Action Committee.

Torkil: I first heard about KAK in 1969. I went to a boarding school in Holbæk, about 65 kilometers from Copenhagen. There was a fellow student, Kim, who was a Maoist. He was a KAK sympathizer and explained Marxism, imperialism, and the parasite state theory to me. It all made perfect sense, and I could recognize much of what he said in everyday life. The theories seemed to explain the world very well. It was obvious that the living conditions of European workers were very different from those of workers in the Third World.

One day, Kim invited Holger to come and talk to us. Holger arrived on his East German motorcycle with short hair and clean clothes—not the typical appearance of young leftists at the time. I was impressed by his commitment and sincerity. In 1971, I joined KUF.

How did KUF relate to KAK?

Jan: KUF was sort of a recruiting ground for KAK. While KAK focused on theory, KUF was more action-oriented. KUF always had more members, too, and at times there were modest attempts at challenging the dominance of KAK—but Gotfred Appel always kept things in check.

How did the Anti-imperialist Action Committee fit in?

Torkil: It provided an arena for direct action. It was quite open and a testing ground for potential KUF and KAK members.

How much influence did Appel have on KUF's journal, Ungkommunisten?

Jan: Not that much, actually. The journal was not censored by Gotfred, if that is what you're asking. However, he made it very clear when something was published that he didn't like.

And his role in Kommunistisk Orientering, *KAK's journal?*

Jan: That was basically his own project. At the same time, one must not underestimate the role of Ulla Hauton, which I think many of us did in the 1970s. She always read and commented on Gotfred's texts and he took her criticism very seriously. The fact that many of us never fully understood the relationship between Gotfred and Ulla certainly contributed to KAK's end in 1978.

In 1972, KAK also founded Tøj til Afrika. How did this project relate to KAK, and how many people were active in it?

Torkil: Nationwide, there were between fifty and sixty people active in TTA. Some only wanted to support liberation movements, others moved on to join KAK. We usually referred to TTA members as "sympathizers."

In a nutshell, what made KAK unique within the left of its time?

Torkil: That certainly was the parasite state theory developed by Gotfred Appel.

What led to the theory?

Torkil: In the 1960s, Gotfred had a Maoist perspective. Many KAK members were sent to work at big companies such as the shipyard Burmeister & Wain, the machine manufacturer FLSmidth, and Tuborg Breweries. The intention was twofold. First, KAK members should study the living conditions of the workers. For example, was it a problem for them when their children needed new shoes or had to go see the dentist? Second, KAK members should try to mobilize the working class on a "nonrevisionist and anti-imperialist" basis. This proved extremely difficult. There was no "single spark that could start a prairie fire"—everything seemed pretty damp.

So, the parasite state theory was a result of KAK's failure to mobilize the working class?

Jan: No, that would be too simple. It was based on studies as well. KAK members knew how high the living standard of the Danish working class was, and we were familiar with Lenin's writings on the labor aristocracy. There was both an empirical and a theoretical angle.

Torkil: Marx and Engels also wrote about the relationship between the English and the Irish working class and illustrated how an imperial working class treats a colonial one. The parasite state theory clearly had reference points in classical Marxism.

Another important influence were ideas formulated during the Chinese Cultural Revolution. Lin Biao, for example, described a revolutionary situation as peasants surrounding towns, which, on a global scale, translated into Third World nations surrounding the imperialist ones ...

So, if you knew all this, why were KAK members send to the factories?

Jan: KAK was still a Marxist organization and the industrial proletariat is central to the Marxist concept of revolution. You didn't want to count out the working class that easily. So, instead of just drawing the obvious conclusions from our analysis, it still needed to be put to test. I would say that the infiltration of the factories was a final attempt to establish a politically productive relationship to the working class. But that didn't happen. It even proved impossible to get workers involved in the Vietnam solidarity movement.

In 1969, KAK got into conflict with the Chinese leadership.

Torkil: That was a matter of analysis. The *Peking Review* published an article celebrating "gigantic revolutionary mass movements" in Western Europe.[2] In response, KAK wrote a letter to the CPC and to the Chinese ambassador in Denmark, stating that this was a completely inaccurate perception and that we had empirical data to prove it. We basically said, "You use the same language to describe what is happening in Indonesia or Vietnam that you use

---

2. The *Peking Review* (since 1979, *Beijing Review*) is the official English-language publication of the government of the People's Republic of China. In the April 30, 1969, issue, which documented the Ninth National Congress of the CPC, Lin Biao wrote: "An unprecedentedly gigantic revolutionary mass movement has broken out in Japan, Western Europe and North America, the 'heartlands' of capitalism" (31).

Left: Cover of the
Peking Review
no. 18, 1969; the
issue was dedicated
to the Ninth National
Congress of the CPC
and contained the cited
article by Lin Biao.

Below: Final paragraph
of a letter sent by
Gotfred Appel to the
Chinese Ambassador
to Copenhagen,
March 29, 1969.

- - - - - - - - - - - - - - -

THIS IS WHAT WE MEAN! WE WANT THE THE NINTH NATIONAL CONGRESS OF
THE CPC, WE WANT CHAIRMAN MAO TO HAVE CORRECT, FULL AND TRUTHFUL INFOR-
MATION ON THE SITUATION IN OUR PART OF THE WORLD ON WHICH TO BASE THEIR
APPRAISAL. WE WARN AGAINST THE INCORRECT, INSUFFICIENT and FALSE IN-
FORMATION ON THIS SITUATION, WHICH WE READ IN ESINHUA NEWS AGENCY§s
NEWS BULLETIN.

    We sincerely hope that this long explanation will help clear up
the misunderstandings presently existing between us!

                With fraternal greetings,
                   K A K

              Political Committee

                (Gotfred Appel)

to describe developments in France or Germany. Why? Those are two very different things." As a result, the official ties to China were cut.

The Vietnam War seems to have played an important role for KAK. How did your experiences from organizing protests against the war influence your politics?

Torkil: The protests confirmed where the Danish working class stood. Those who came to the demonstrations were young people and students, not workers.

Jan: This wasn't unique to Denmark of course. In the U.S., antiwar demonstrations were even attacked by trade unionists. Our experiences in the factories were telling. When we handed out flyers about antiwar demonstrations, we got no response at all. The workers were interested in higher wages, not international politics. They were led by the representatives of the labor aristocracy, the DKP and the trade unions.

Torkil: The DKP, for example, controlled the *Sømændenes forbund*, a seamen's union. During the Vietnam War, the union was quite happy to ship supplies to the American troops in Saigon, as long as its members had their wages doubled for sailing into high-risk zones.

What was the class background of KAK's members?

Torkil: Both working class and middle class. My father was a ferry navigator and my mother a nurse. Holger's father was a carpenter, Niels's father was a bookkeeper. The standard of living of my family increased enormously at the end of the 1950s—we could afford a house, a car, and holidays in Italy and Spain.

Jan: My father was a firefighter and my mother worked different factory jobs. I have two older brothers, both of whom are craftsmen. I was the first one in my family to get a high school diploma.

Quite a few KUF members also held working-class jobs. Peter Døllner was a carpenter, Holger Jensen a firefighter. Gotfred Appel drove a taxi for a few years, before KAK provided a modest salary for him and Ulla.

Let us continue with KAK's history: once it was clear that the working class of the imperialist countries no longer qualified as a revolutionary subject, you turned to the masses of the Third World. Is that correct?

Jan: Our reasoning can be summed up in four steps:

1. The capitalists of the imperialist countries made huge profits, *super profits*, by exploiting the Third World. Later, we used the theory of unequal exchange to further this analysis.[3]
2. The superprofits were not freely distributed to the workers of the First World. Capitalism does not distribute anything freely. However, the superprofits created social conditions, in which workers, led by Social Democratic parties, fought for pieces of the pie. At times, it needed long and hard struggles to get those pieces, but during those struggles the labor aristocracy was formed.
3. Over time, the interests of the capitalist class and the working class in the imperialist countries became more and more alike. The primary interest of the workers was to keep their jobs, and hence a strong capitalist economy, even if that meant fighting imperialist wars.
4. As a result, the workers of the imperialist countries did not side with the workers and peasants of the Third World, but with those who gave them jobs, namely the Western capitalists. On a psychological and social level, the workers never were our enemies, though. Most individuals follow their objective interests.

So, how come some don't? Like, apparently, you?

Jan: Of course there is always a difference between the situation of an individual and the situation of a class; or, between psychology and sociology, if you will. There is a possibility for individuals to act against the objective short-term interests of their class. But these individuals will always be a minority and even for them it needs special circumstances.

---

3. See "It Is All About Politics" in this volume.

Torkil: The special circumstances in our case were provided by the unique situation at the end of the 1960s. Social protest movements in the imperialist countries, liberation movements in the colonized countries, and a widespread belief in a better world opened a window for us. And then there was KAK right here in Denmark, which provided a concrete possibility for revolutionary organizing. This was a strong cocktail.

But to be clear: as an individual you can never completely leave the objective conditions of your life behind. In 1974, we published a book, in which guerrilla fighters from Angola told their stories. It was called "Victory or Death."[4] That was not our reality. We could always make choices. Your socialization always catches up with you. Today I like to say that I can feel neoliberalism running in my blood, too ...

I'm sure we will get to neoliberalism. But let us stick to the "unique situation" of the late 1960s for a moment. You have mentioned "the belief in a better world" and the "concrete possibility for revolutionary organizing." What did you expect to happen?

Torkil: Our view of revolutionary development was simple. In 1969–1970 there were about forty liberation movements active in Latin America, Asia, and Africa. The Vietnamese struggle was heading towards victory, and it looked good for many others as well. The rhetoric of most movements was anti-imperialist and socialist. They vowed to put an end to capitalist superprofits. This opened up the prospect for a fundamental crisis of capitalism with huge effects for both the capitalist class and the working class of the imperialist countries, which, in turn, promised to create the necessary conditions for a global uprising. What can I say? We had a very deterministic view of history.

---

4. *Sejre eller dø: 4 angolesere beretter om deres vej til revolution* [Victory or Death: Four Angolans Tell about Their Way to the Revolution] (Copenhagen: Futura, 1974) was based on stories from the book *The Revolution in Angola: MPLA Life Histories and Documents*, edited by the LSM founder Don Barnett and Roy Harvey (Indianapolis: Bobbs-Merrill, 1972). For Barnett and the LSM, see later sections of the interview and the appendix.

Jan: We basically considered the Marxist analysis of capitalism's necessary downfall to be a natural law. We were very scientifically oriented. Our positions were based on social study and economic analysis, not on psychology and wishful thinking. Our tools were investigation and reflection. We wanted to identify the laws that would lead the system into a severe crisis. Whether we ever achieved that is a different question.

Torkil: On an organizational level, the goal was to form a group able to understand the historical process and act when it became necessary. That was the purpose of KAK. We did not have a detailed analysis of what would happen in ten or twenty years, but we were convinced that we needed to be prepared for action. We wanted to prepare the future revolutionary party, and supporting liberation movements was a way to speed up the revolutionary process. Essentially, we were pursuing two things at the same time: one, building a strong organization; two, supporting liberation movements. Illegal activities would soon be part of this. But to focus entirely on illegal work was not in the cards for us. To go underground and openly declare war on the state would have been a lost cause. The state would have crushed us within six months.

Jan: To have a legal anti-imperialist practice was also important for recruiting sympathizers. We never looked for mass membership, but we still needed a support network and tried to find the right people.

Torkil: We must add, though, that our support for liberation movements was not only based on ideology. It had a strong practical and economic aspect as well. At the time, socialism was widely considered the economic system that would guarantee the improvement of living conditions in the Third World: better education, better health care, etc. Many experiences confirmed this—one just had to compare the situation in Cuba to the one in Haiti.

Furthermore, there was international solidarity. The Cubans, for example, provided enormous material support for African liberation movements. Literally thousands of Cubans went to Angola to support the MPLA. This had a strong impact on world affairs. Nelson Mandela's release from Robben Island and the subsequent political changes in South Africa were directly related to the Cuban involvement in the region. A lot can be said about the

Cuban regime, but its internationalist orientation was genuine. Cuba did not profit politically or economically from its engagement in Africa.

Another example is the relationship between the Soviet Union and China before the Sino-Soviet split. In the 1950s, the Soviet Union provided China with blueprints for the production of everything from toothbrushes to long-range ballistic missiles. They trained thousands of Chinese engineers. This was crucial to China's economic development. In this case, there were political conditions of course, but the main motivation was still the expansion of socialism. We believed that this was the way forward for all Third World countries.

The impact that Lenin's "Imperialism, the Highest Stage of Capitalism" had on KAK's analysis of imperialism seems pretty obvious.

Jan: KAK's reference points were always the classical texts of Marxism-Leninism. As far as imperialism was concerned, everything circled around Lenin's text. This didn't even change when our empirical studies in the 1970s showed that its analysis was no longer applicable: Lenin's theories on monopolization, finance capital, foreign direct investments, etc., could no longer explain the enormous gaps in wealth. But it needed KAK's demise and the founding of M-KA for us to be able to improve our analysis.

Torkil: It's actually quite amazing that such a short and somewhat muddled text, written hastily in a Swiss library with limited access to source material, could be regarded as the *ne plus ultra* in the Marxist analysis of imperialism for over half a century. It really shows the position that Lenin had within the left and the power of Soviet propaganda.

What was life like as a KAK member?

Torkil: We were a very disciplined and hard-working group. Politics came before your personal career or your personal interests, often enough your family. During long periods of time we were "voluntarily unemployed" in order to entirely focus on political work. Those of us who were active in Tøj til Afrika, like myself, collected clothes, sorted and packed them, and drove around to collect things for the flea markets. In the summer holidays, we also

TA' PÅ KLUNSERLEJR I DIN SOMMERFERIE

STØT BEFRIELSESBEVÆGELSERNE I DEN 3. VERDEN

FORENINGEN TØJ TIL AFRIKA

"Come to the Ragpickers' Camp during Summer Holidays: Support Liberation Movements in the Third World—Tøj til Afrika project" (ca. 1980).

organized two-week Tøj til Afrika camps, which introduced new people to the organization. With KAK, we had a study circle once a week to discuss theoretical problems. Personally, I wrote articles and formulated drafts for position papers. There was also the publishing and printing work, and not least the illegal practice, which was very time-consuming. It was not just about planning and executing different actions, but it also included numerous trite tasks: paying rent, moving cars, organizing equipment, etc. And during all of this you had to make sure that you weren't under observation. Yet, as stressful as it was, after a few years it became a part of everyday life—although the stress always returned before a bigger action, that was never just routine.

All in all, though, I have good memories of the time in KAK. It was satisfying to be engaged in a practice that corresponded to your theory.

Jan: Commitment was crucial—you were available for the organization around the clock. If your contribution was needed, you didn't hesitate and went to work. I remember that I once got home after midnight on New Year's Eve. Understandably, my wife wasn't happy. She was a Tøj til Afrika member but not part of KAK. She didn't know about the illegal work, and so I couldn't explain to her that we had been out for shooting practice. New Year's Eve was a good night for it because of all the fireworks, but Gotfred Appel got arrested when the police found ammunition in his car during a random check.

Jan Weimann in the Vridsløselille State Prison, 1994.

We had to take care of the situation, and so I got back late. Such incidents were always difficult to deal with and dividing time between KAK and my family was a constant challenge. On several occasions, my wife knew that something was wrong, but I could never tell her what it was. Once I got stuck in Lebanon during the civil war after visiting the PFLP, because the airport in Beirut had been shut down. Holger visited my wife, told her that I was in Norway suffering from pneumonia, and asked her to call and excuse me at work. I kept a part-time job, which allowed me to make significant financial contributions to KAK during the first few years.

How did your wife take it when you were arrested in 1989?

Jan: I was together with my second wife then—who didn't know anything about my illegal activities either. The arrest came as a shock to her, and it was not an easy situation to deal with. But I got another chance, which was very important for me, also because it allowed me to see my daughter regularly while I was in prison.

The Sino-Soviet conflict and the Anti-imperialist Perspective

You have mentioned the Sino-Soviet conflict, which bitterly divided the Marxist left during the 1970s. While KAK embraced the Chinese line in the 1960s, you've already mentioned the falling-out with Beijing at the end of the decade. At the same time, you've lauded the internationalism of the Soviet Union. Was this the side you were taking?

Torkil: No. What I said before concerned exclusively the Soviet Union's foreign policy—and even there, we would have wanted the Soviet government to be more radical and stronger in its support of Third World liberation movements. Regarding the country's political and economic system, we had no sympathies at all. In the so-called "real socialism," a "democratic economy" meant "nationalization," which, in turn, meant that the state apparatus owned all the means of production. However, just because the state apparatus owns the means of production, the mode of production doesn't necessarily change. The mode of production in the Soviet Union was very similar to capitalist ones, and sometimes worse. Look at the *Volkseigene Betriebe*, the so-called "Publically Owned Companies," in the former East Germany: people never felt that they were really in charge. It was the state that was in charge, and the people were not the state. The planned economy of the Soviet Union and its Eastern European allies was not democratic but very hierarchical. That's why the Soviet Union was never a model for us. However, it was a tactical ally in the support of liberation movements. One must not forget that the simple existence of the Soviet Union as a global superpower was very important for them. It created a space for them to become active. Had it not been for the Soviet Union, the U.S. might have used nuclear weapons to wipe out the Vietnamese resistance. Without the international balance of power guaranteed by the Soviet Union—also with regard to armament—things would have looked very different.

Jan: Ideologically, we found ourselves in a dilemma. We did see the Cultural Revolution in China as a positive attempt to revise communism, but China was no ally in the support of liberation movements. In that respect, the progressive force was the Soviet Union. It had an objective interest in the liberation movements' success and in the global expansion of socialism. Its leaders also chose their allies wisely. Their criteria were very similar to ours: they were looking for socialist movements with popular support. The Chinese leadership, on the other hand, was so hostile towards the Soviet Union that it basically supported anyone who shared that sentiment. China developed ties to the most obscure political groups, and its foreign policy began to border on the absurd. In Angola, for example, they supported UNITA and worked alongside the CIA.

Torkil: In the late 1970s and early 1980s, China held the position that the Soviet Union was the most dangerous of all imperialist powers, and they encouraged the liberation movements to side with Western European nations and the U.S. As Jan said, it all became pretty grotesque, and it also changed the perception of China among many liberation movements and their allies. KAK was far from the only organization that had a falling-out with the CPC around that time. If you go back to the early 1970s, the PFLP was very pro-Chinese and hugely inspired by Mao's guerrilla strategies. They were not very close to the Soviet Union. All this changed within the next decade.

Jan: However, as Torkil said, we did not take any side in the Sino-Soviet conflict as such and stayed away from the ideological debates and polemics.

Notable African socialists, for example Julius Nyerere, also tried to avoid these debates. Was this a factor in the relations you developed with African liberation movements?

Jan: I wouldn't say so. We were primarily concerned with the conditions for the liberation struggle in a specific country, not with ideological subtleties or postrevolution development strategies. Our discussions with liberation movements focused on the analysis of the current political and economic system and the possibilities to attack it.

Our approach to the development of socialism in Western Europe was similar. We weren't very concerned with Denmark's socialist future, much more with the downfall of Danish capitalism.

Torkil: Strategic questions were very important to us. That's why we did not want to support the PFLP–Special Operations or other groups that focused on spectacular international actions. We were more interested in a practice rooted in popular mass movements.

Can you tell us more about how you decided to support particular movements? You have made your criteria clear, but how did you get the information required to make the relevant decisions? Did you meet with representatives of all the movements you were interested in supporting?

Jan: Not at first. There were so many liberation movements, it was impossible to have direct contact with them all. We began by looking at what they had written about their theory and practice.

Torkil: Information was spread in different ways at the time. There was no Internet in 1970. However, we had a subscription to the BBC World Service, which allowed us to follow the political developments in many countries on a daily basis. We always tried to have a good understanding of a particular movement before we considered supporting it. Even if we weren't that concerned with ideological subtleties, common political ground was crucial. Everything else followed from there.

Another aspect that was important was the degree of support that a particular movement already had. One of the organizations we supported, the PFLOAG/PFLO in Oman, was small and did not get much outside support, so for them a million Danish crowns really made a difference. That was not necessarily the case for organizations like the ANC in South Africa.

Jan: One could say that we had three different ways of supporting movements: some we supported legally through Tøj til Afrika; some we supported illegally; and some we supported both legally and—to a smaller degree—illegally, but without telling them. The PFLP knew what we were doing, but none of the other movements did. ZANU, for example, got resources that we acquired illegally, but they were unaware of it. Many liberation movements were infiltrated by intelligence services, and we did not want to take any risks.

The PFLP

Out of all the organizations you worked with, you obviously had the closest ties to the PFLP. Why?

Jan: The PFLP had a strong Marxist-Leninist commitment and we were very impressed with their analysis. Slogans like "Our enemies are imperialism, Zionism, and Arab reactionaries" spoke to us. Their outlook was very close to ours. Furthermore, they fought in a strategically important part of the world. Middle Eastern politics are about oil. That's what makes the region so valuable for imperialism as well as for the fight against it. If no more oil flows from the Middle East to the Western world, then capitalism will have severe problems.

PFLOAG guerrilla fighter in Oman, early 1970s.

Torkil: The PFLP's pan-Arab approach was also crucial for us. The primary objective of the PFLP wasn't the liberation of Palestine—globally speaking, that's rather irrelevant. The struggle for Palestine has a high symbolic value, but its geopolitical importance is limited. Instead, the PFLP followed the pan-Arab visions of Nasser and others.[5] A socialist future should engulf the entire Arab world from Syria to Morocco. That's why the PFLP had cells in many countries, including Saudi Arabia. In general, the PFLP had a strong internationalist outlook. It allowed liberation movements from around the world to use its facilities. During my visits, I saw Kurds, Turks, Iranians, South Africans, and Nicaraguans. In other words, supporting the PFLP meant to support many liberation movements. Finally, the PFLP was a well-established organization with a lot of potential. It had a proper army with training camps, it ran clinics and children's homes, even a pension system.

How did you first get in touch with the PFLP?

Jan: Through Palestinians living in Malmö, Sweden. Eventually, KAK members traveled to the Middle East, and we continued to have regular meetings.

Soon after you had established contact with the PFLP, there were several splits within the organization. How did that affect you?

Torkil: Especially after the so-called Black September,[6] a discussion emerged within the PFLP about popular mass mobilization on the one hand and international operations, that is, high-profile hijackings and the like, on the other. George Habash, the more traditional Marxist, stressed the former, Wadi Haddad the latter. This was probably the most important split that occurred, but it was a friendly one. The two lines existed parallel to one another for several years.

We chose to work with Habash. To this day, people associate us with

---

5. Gamel Abdal Nasser served as Egypt's president from 1956 until his death in 1970. He was one of most prominent proponents of pan-Arab ideas.

6. "Black September" refers to the armed conflicts between the Jordanian government and Palestinian organizations in Jordan in September 1970, causing the death of over three thousand Palestinians. See also "It Is All About Politics" in this volume.

Haddad, but that's only because we already had contact with him before the split, and so he knew about us. That's why Carlos, who ended up working closely with Haddad, also knew about us, but we never met Carlos, let alone collaborated with him. All of those rumors are nonsense. We were never interested in anything of that kind, nor were we ever interested in contacts with intelligence services, which Carlos had plenty of. We stayed as far away from them as possible, whether they were Libyan, Lebanese, Syrian, or Iraqi—or the STASI, for that matter. We had no sympathies for the states they worked for, and, sooner or later, intelligence services always betray you. They have their own agenda, and it is usually very different from yours.

But how could the intelligence services not know about your meetings with the PFLP? Where did they take place?

Jan: In the beginning, the meetings took place in Denmark. However, we did not feel comfortable with that, because the PFLP representatives always used local PFLP members as escorts who, in our opinion, presented security issues. For example, they used phones that we knew weren't safe. Considering that, PET was probably aware of our meetings back then.

Later, we traveled to the Middle East, but that was also risky because of international intelligence services, and because the Danish authorities were always suspicious about people traveling to the region. On one occasion, Holger was followed by agents directly from the airport upon returning to Denmark.

Finally, we ended up having most of the meetings in Eastern Europe. Both we and the PFLP could travel there easily, while it was a difficult region for PET to operate in—they couldn't do much even if they had information about the meetings taking place. Usually, we met in Sofia or Budapest, but also in East Berlin. At first, we simply crossed at Checkpoint Charlie, but we always had our documents photocopied there, so we started to take the ferry from Southern Denmark to Rostock. There were plenty of left-wing Danes who went to East Germany for vacation, so it was easy to blend in. We never had any problems at the border and were never approached by STASI agents. They might have had an eye on our meetings, but if there ever were any records they've been destroyed—nothing has surfaced since the collapse of the East German state.

In general, communication with the PFLP became increasingly professional after we reestablished contact following the KAK split in 1978. From that point on, we had regular and reliable contacts. Before that, we were always met by different people, who did not always have a clear understanding of the work we did and of our security needs. I mean, when you're met by an iconic aircraft hijacker in a hotel lobby in Sofia, it doesn't exactly help you to remain unnoticed.

What documents were you traveling with?

Torkil: Our own passports, although we had more than one.

Jan: Especially when we held our meetings in the Middle East, we needed to change passports regularly. Once the meetings were held in Eastern Europe, things were considerably easier.

Did you have contacts with DFLP members as well? It seems that their line would have been close to yours, with a strong focus on popular uprisings and reservations towards high-profile actions.

Torkil: In theory, you are right, but in practice they were a small and intellectual group. We perceived them as akin to many left-wing groups in Europe. They did not have the mass base that the PFLP had. So although there was some contact, there was no close collaboration.

Jan: The first two KUF groups that traveled to the Middle East had meetings with both the PFLP and the DFLP. Another important reason for us choosing to work with the PFLP was that it had a much stronger presence in the occupied territories. In Gaza, they were the single biggest organization.

Alleged connections to the RAF

It seems important to you not to be confused with European urban guerrilla movements of the 1970s, like the Red Army Faction in Germany. Can you explain this?

Torkil: We had different politics and a different practice. We also had different backgrounds. The youth rebellions of the late 1960s, which seemed important for the formation of many of the urban guerrilla movements, were of little importance to us. It seems to me that for RAF members, the rebellion on the private level was very central. Politics and private life, including the relationship to your family, your living arrangements, etc., were considered to be closely linked. In KAK, we didn't see things that way. We were strongly rooted in Marxist-Leninist cadre politics. This was an aspect that Gotfred Appel had brought to the organization from his long experience in communist parties. Discipline was key—and so was patience. Many of the urban guerrilla movements wanted revolutionary change here and now. We pursued a long-term strategy.

Furthermore, our practice was "invisible" with regard to Danish society. We were not at war with the Danish state and did not send out communiqués after our actions. We used illegal means that looked like ordinary crime to support Third World liberation movements. That's very different to the urban guerrilla groups, which attacked European states head-on. We saw that strategy as suicidal, because, according to our analysis, there was no chance of winning. There was no mass base. If we had tried something similar in Denmark, we would have been finished very quickly. Instead, we wanted to be an ally to Third World liberation movements for many years. We managed at least twenty. That also meant that we were still supporting liberation struggles at a time when most urban guerrilla groups had vanished or were entirely on the defensive. They were *underground* revolutionaries and anti-imperialists, we were *undercover* ones.

Jan: An example that illustrates our history comes from the protests against the 1970 World Bank congress in Copenhagen. Gotfred and Ulla were in Jordan at the time, meeting with the PFLP. KUF members were meant to participate in the protests, but not to engage in rioting and open confrontation with the police, but instead to do some direct action targeting the venue and the delegates. However, one thing led to another, and suddenly we were caught up in heavy streetfighting, Molotov cocktails were thrown, etc. When Gotfred and Ulla returned to Denmark, they were furious. They called us immature and adventurist. We were summoned to the school bench, so to speak, and told to read Marx's *Capital*, Lenin, and so on.

It seems to me that many of the people who joined the urban guerrilla movements were very action-driven and never had any such experience. I mean, don't get me wrong, we were action-driven, too, but we had someone who challenged us when our actions weren't productive.

Why were you criticized for the rioting during the protests against the World Bank congress, but not during the protests against the screening of The Green Berets?

Jan: We had decided on different strategies. With *The Green Berets*, the goal was to stop the screening, and anything that contributed to that was fine. With the World Bank congress, fighting the police didn't seem very productive. We had decided to disrupt the meeting with targeted actions. Therefore, the involvement in the rioting was seen as a lack of discipline. Furthermore, some stupid mistakes were made that attracted the attention of the authorities—like leaving Molotov cocktails laying around the KAK print shop.

Let us quickly return to the urban guerrilla groups: You haven't met any of them in training camps in the Middle East either?

Torkil: This is one of the rumors that never go away. People seem to find this idea very exciting. We have visited such camps, but we never went through any training there. Why should we? What was it that that we could learn at a camp in Lebanon? We wanted to do illegal work in Denmark. Of course, they can teach you how to dismantle a gun and how to put it back together, but you can learn that in Denmark, too. Most of the other things you could learn in those camps were irrelevant to us. We didn't need to cross desert borders in the middle of the night, we needed to know how to rent safe apartments, how to protect ourselves against surveillance, how to stake out targets for possible actions, how to do robberies without leaving a trace, and so on.

Undercover work requires a detailed knowledge of the society you operate in. We had to learn these things ourselves.

Besides, we consciously avoided contact with other Europeans when we were in the Middle East, and this included the training camps. We considered contacts to underground movements in Europe, especially those with imprisoned members, a major risk.

Jan: There was also an aspect of principle. We went to the Middle East to offer support to organizations, not to ask for any. The urban guerrilla groups had a different kind of relationship to them.

Where do all the rumors come from that you had contacts with the RAF and with Carlos?

Torkil: I think it's mainly media hype; it is part of a story that the media tries to sell. I suppose that's how things work, but I find it disappointing when presumably progressive journalists do the exact same thing. For example, there were two people in Denmark who provided logistic support to the RAF. They organized passports and hid some RAF members, including Andreas Baader, in a summer house on the west coast of Jutland, I believe.[7] To this day, it is unclear who these people were, but it's been suggested repeatedly that we had something to do with it, which is bunk.

It has been suggested that explosives from the Swedish army's weapons depot in Flen were used in a failed 1988 attack on the NATO base in Rota, Spain, allegedly executed by former RAF members.

Jan: I don't know if that was the case or not. There were no conditions tied to the support we gave to the PFLP, whether it was money, weapons, or explosives. We had set up a weapons cache in France that the PFLP had access to, and whatever happened with the materials from there, we don't know. The cache itself was eventually discovered by French police after a tip from an informant.

Our plans to smuggle the weapons we got in Flen to Israel were never

---

7. Jutland is the mainland part of Denmark, bordering Germany.

realized. We thought about traveling there as surfers, hiding weapons in our boards, but also about shipping bulldozers with weapons concealed inside them. In the end, however, all of those plans seemed too risky. Had we got caught, it would have probably meant the end of our activities and years in Israeli prisons. This was not something we wanted to risk, and not a risk that we wanted to expose anyone else to either. I mean, we couldn't just ask someone to transport a surfboard with antitank missiles to Israel, could we?

I suppose not. Perhaps especially not since you had thirty-four of them. The surfboard found at the Blekingegade apartment contained two. That would have meant many trips to Israel ...

Jan: That's why we had the idea with the bulldozers. Anyway, we simply were ill-prepared for the weapons situation. When we were in Flen, we basically just grabbed whatever we could. Then most of them ended up at the Blekingegade apartment and were a major headache.

There have also been suggestions that Holger gathered intelligence for the Landshut hijacking in 1977.[8] Peter Øvig Knudsen writes about this extensively in his book.

Torkil: Well, we weren't Holger's guardians, so we can't say what he did and didn't do, but this is extremely—and I mean *extremely*—unlikely. The Landshut hijacking did not fit in with KAK's approach, politically, strategically, or tactically. Holger was a disciplined "party soldier." It's very hard to believe that he would have decided to do such a thing on his own, and it would have never been condoned by KAK. Gotfred Appel would have gone berserk. Furthermore, we went through the emotionally very draining anti–gender discrimination campaign in 1977, which eventually led to KAK's demise. Holger was strongly affected by it. So, even emotionally, he wouldn't have been able to do this at the time. And if he had nonetheless, I'm sure he would have told us about it at some point. Finally, how is he supposed to have been recruited? At that point, we no longer collaborated with Haddad. We had even lost contact with the PFLP.

---

8. See "It Is All About Politics," page 46 in this volume.

Øvig Knudsen suggests that Haddad talked to him during the KAK leadership's visit to Baghdad in early 1977.

Jan: What Øvig Knudsen didn't know was that I was also in Baghdad at the time. He assumed it was only Gotfred, Ulla, and Holger. It is true that we met Haddad on two occasions when we were there, but both times all four of us were present. During the entire visit, we stayed in the same house on the outskirts of Baghdad and couldn't travel into the city because we had no proper papers. Hence, it would have been impossible for Holger to arrange a separate meeting. Besides, you must not underestimate how disciplined an organization KAK was. We are talking about a strong internalization of principles. Nobody even dreamed about going behind the back of the leadership, Holger included.

Okay, one more theory that has been thrown around: you were linked to Danmarks Socialistiske Befrielseshær, or "Denmark's Socialist Liberation Army," a group that claimed responsibility for a series of arson attacks against corporate targets around Århus in the early 1980s.

Torkil: That's also nonsense. No one has ever found out who those people were, and we don't know who they were either. The name alone tells you that they had nothing to do with us. "Denmark's Socialist Liberation Army"? What did they want to liberate Denmark from? We were staunchly antinationalistic and rejected all forms of left-wing national romanticism. Already in 1972, KAK was the only left-wing organization in Denmark that didn't protest the country becoming a member of the European Community, the European Union's predecessor. Why should it be more likely that the working class in a small country like Denmark made revolution than a united European working class? The baggage of nationalist romanticism in the European left is heavy. That's one of the reasons why it's so ironic that we were accused of romanticizing national liberation struggles—even if it is true that we underestimated the nationalist element in them.

There were also militant groups in Western Europe whose members did not live underground, for example Germany's Revolutionary Cells. Did you see more similarities to them? Did you follow their activities at all?

Jan: Not really. Although there were perhaps similarities in strategy, the political outlook, the objective of the struggle, and, perhaps most importantly, the context were too different. Yes, both Denmark and Germany were parasite states, but the differences were considerable. Germany had to come to terms with the history of the Nazi regime and the Holocaust in very different ways than Denmark, which was occupied by the Nazis during the war. That German state and the Danish state were very different and acted in different ways. The manner in which they reacted to the protests of the late 1960s illustrates this. In Germany, the security forces were much more brutal. The images from the Shah's visit in 1967 were shocking to most Danes.[9] This also called for a different political response. It was not up to us to decide what the response should look like in Germany. We were focused on Denmark.

It is important to note that we in no way want to condemn or discredit the German comrades, even if we might have seen certain things differently. They fought under specific conditions and did what they considered right. And some of their actions we could get behind fully, such as the attacks on U.S. army bases during the Vietnam War. This was a concrete interference with the imperialist war machine. We might have considered similar things—however, there were no U.S. army bases in Denmark.

Torkil: Another important difference is that due to our "invisible strategy" we lacked the fairly wide circles of sympathizers and supporters the German groups had. We were small and weren't able to engage in high-profile actions. Hence, our impact was smaller, too.

Jan: Well, it depends on what you mean by "impact." As far as an impact on the state or on European society is concerned, yes, our impact doesn't compare to theirs—I still remember the "Wanted" posters at every German gas station I stopped at in the 1970s. The German groups were looking for a confrontation with the state, and the state responded accordingly. In that

---

9. In June 1967, Mohammad Reza Pahlavi, the Shah of Iran, visited Germany. German and Iranian security forces violently attacked anti-Shah demonstrations. On June 2, the student Benno Ohnesorg was shot dead by a policeman—the name of the urban guerrilla group Movement Second of June (*Bewegung 2. Juni*) refers to this incident.

sense, their impact was very strong. But in terms of supporting liberation movements, I think ours was stronger. We provided quite a few of them with significant resources.

In 1982, the RAF published a text entitled "The Guerrilla, the Resistance, and the Anti-Imperialist Front," suggesting the formation of an anti-imperialist front in Western Europe.[10] Did that debate interest you at all?

Jan: Not really. We still considered such ideas unrealistic. Besides, it had no practical relevance for us. As we have already noted, any kind of collaboration with the RAF or similar groups would have been a major security risk. Not for them, they were already underground—but for us, since we had chosen a different strategy.

How about relationships to legal Marxist organizations in Germany?

Torkil: We didn't find much common ground there either. In 1974, four KAK members moved to Frankfurt, where they lived and worked in a factory for a year. Their aim was to study the social and economic conditions in Germany and the state of the working class. When they returned, they wrote a critical piece about the German Marxist-Leninist groups, particularly the KBW.[11]

You have stressed in your writings that you weren't completely isolated within the Western European left. In particular, you've mentioned collaboration with groups in Sweden and Norway. Can you tell us about these groups?

Jan: We had fairly close contact to an internationalist group in Sweden called Aurora. They mainly did propaganda work for liberation movements and also

---

10. The text is included in J. Smith and André Moncourt (eds.), *The Red Army Faction: A Documentary History. Volume 2: Dancing with Imperialism* (Oakland: PM Press, 2013), and available online at http://www.germanguerilla.com. The German original was published in 1982 as "Guerilla, Widerstand und anti-imperialistische Front."

11. "Intet kan bygges på illusioner" [Nothing Can Be Built on Illusions] in *Kommunistisk Orientering* no. 4, 1975.

translated some KAK articles into Swedish. Furthermore, they were active in the Swedish Emmaus movement, which, like Tøj til Afrika, supported liberation movements with money, clothes, shoes, and medicine.[12] In Norway, we were in contact with a small group that did some publishing work.

Other than that, there weren't many groups in Europe that shared our perspective, only individuals here and there. I wouldn't say that we were isolated within the European left, but we certainly didn't share the outlook of most left-wing organizations at the time. We saw most of them fighting for higher wages for European workers; something we considered reactionary. In Denmark, the further you went to the left, the higher the demands became: the DKP wanted two extra crowns per hour, the KFML ten, and so on. We didn't want to have anything to do with that. For us, such an approach only fastened the ties between Danish workers and the capitalists, at the cost of the exploited people of the Third World. We were clear about this, so it's probably not surprising that many on the left turned against us. Well, we might have asked for it, too. We weren't very shy in our criticism, we were very antagonistic. Which probably comes naturally if you're convinced that you alone are right ...

Which you were?

Jan: Yes, KAK was very elitist.

Torkil: We were used to Leninist rhetoric, pure and simple. We were no Kautskys or Bernsteins. Calling other leftists "idiots" and "traitors" came easily. With this in mind, the hostile reactions probably really weren't that much of a surprise.

---

12. Emmaus is an international solidarity organization providing material aid to the poor and homeless. Founded in France in 1949, local groups have a high degree of independence. There are several Emmaus groups active in Sweden today.

The Liberation Support Movement, the Black Panthers, and the Weather Underground

It seems that the strongest collaboration you had with any Western political group was with the Liberation Support Movement in North America. How did you first get in touch with them?

Jan: I'm actually not sure. I think it was simply through reading some of their texts, liking them, and getting in touch. Then, in 1970, Peter Døllner spent half a year in Canada, establishing close ties to them. I also met Don Barnett, the LSM founder, in Tanzania in 1972. Then we had very regular contact throughout the 1970s, before the LSM dissolved in 1982. Barnett himself died in 1975.

Torkil: I don't recall the details either, but the connection dates back to the early 1970s. We had a very similar background: Maoism, the resistance against the war in Vietnam, and the support of liberation movements. There were also similarities on the organizational level: we were both small,

Left: *LSM News* Summer 1975—LSM founder Don Barnett had recently died; right: a publication by the LSM Information Center, 1974.

121

professional, and disciplined groups with a strong, charismatic leader. In the case of the LSM, this was the aforementioned Don Barnett, an anthropologist who had written the books *Mau Mau from Within*, telling the story of the Kenyan resistance movement against British imperialism, and *With the Guerrillas in Angola*, an account of the MPLA. Both organizations also had the same practical focus, namely the material support of liberation movements. The LSM made a huge contribution to spreading information about liberation movements in North America, especially by publishing *Life Histories* from the struggle, which opened the eyes of many North Americans.[13]

Jan: It was encouraging to see an organization in North America whose approach was so similar to ours, and it also helped us prove to other European leftists that our analysis wasn't unique for an organization from the imperialist world.

Did you have any disagreements with the LSM?

Jan: They were much more critical of the Black Panthers than we were. We had many sympathies with the Panthers' struggle and published a number of articles about them. But these differences didn't have much of an impact on our collaboration. We simply avoided the most sensitive issues.

What were the differences in your respective perceptions of the Black Panthers?

Jan: The LSM saw them as swashbuckling coffee shop socialists. I guess, they also saw no progressive potential in what was often considered "black isolationism." Of course, the LSM had much better conditions for studying the Black Panthers than we did, but we hoped that they would weaken the military engagement of the U.S. in the Third World. Admittedly, though, in this case our view was based more on hope than scientific analysis.

---

13. The series *Life Histories from the Revolution*, published by the LSM Information Center in the 1970s, included autobiographical accounts of revolutionaries from Angola, South Africa, Namibia, Zimbabwe, and Kenya.

In False Nationalism, False Internationalism, *the authors E. Tani and Kaé Sera criticize the LSM for tying their support for liberation movements to certain conditions.*[14] *Tani and Sera mention examples of white LSM members visiting FRELIMO camps in Mozambique and evaluating them politically, which was considered a neocolonial gesture. What do you make of this critique?*

Jan: I'm not sure what LSM members did during their visits to Africa, so I can't say much about that. However, I do understand that you want to learn as much as you can about a movement you support. If you only have limited support to give, of course you want it to go to the right place; you want it to be a positive contribution and to make a difference. If you have several movements to choose from, you need to make the right decision.

Torkil: I think it's also important to differentiate between learning something about movements and demanding something from movements. We always tried to learn about them, but we never made demands. Once we gave them a million crowns, it was entirely up to them to decide what to do with the money. They knew best what they needed it for. Whether it went to medicine, plane tickets, or machine guns was none of our concern.

Jan: The impression I got from the LSM was that they worked on similar principles. We also wrote reports about the refugee camps we visited and collected as much information as we could. What I can say with certainty about the LSM is that its members were very committed and that they provided much-needed support. They had plenty of technological equipment and related knowhow, especially when it came to printing facilities and radio communication systems.

When you chose the movements you supported, how important was the strategic factor? You have said that you were particularly interested in struggles that were of strategic significance for the overall fight against imperialism. One could argue that this easily leads to an instrumentalization

---

14. E. Tani and Kaé Sera, *False Nationalism False Internationalism: Class Contradictions in the Armed Struggle* (Chicago: Seeds Beneath the Snow, 1985).

of movements: it is not so much their struggle per se that is of interest, but whether it fits in with the revolutionary master plan of Western vanguardists.

Torkil: To a certain degree, you are right. In this respect, our deterministic world view didn't help much. We were know-it-alls who thought we could make very general assessments. After 1978, things changed, however. Our personal connections to people active in the liberation movements and our knowledge about their situation and the conditions of their struggle also increased. We became less abstract in our understanding of the world and overall more humble.

In the North American context, it has often been argued that colonialism and imperialism also have an internal dimension. People speak of "oppressed nations" in the U.S. and Canada, something that doesn't really happen in the European context. Did you ever discuss this with LSM members?

Jan: I don't remember any extended discussions about this. Of course we were aware that the conditions in North America were different from those in Denmark and the rest of Europe. Racism and the oppression and exploitation of the indigenous population played a different role. That's why we saw revolutionary potential in the struggle of the Black Panthers. We hadn't really researched the status and support they had in the black community, but they were certainly more interesting to us than white movements competing in revolutionary phraseology.

UNGKOMMUNISTEN

De undertrykte og sultende vil sejre!

MAJ 1970   3. ÅRG. NR. 4

At the same time, we didn't have the impression that the revolutionary potential of the North American movements were on par with the struggle in Angola or Mozambique. That was also true for the indigenous resistance. It seemed unlikely to us that the American Indian Movement would be able to start a revolution. It had very little support from the American working class. Of course we were in solidarity with their struggle, but we mainly saw it as a tragic one. It seemed similar to the situation in Greenland, which we also analyzed. We published articles about Greenland in *Ungkommunisten*, but we didn't see much revolutionary potential there either. In the U.S., the brutal state repression of both the American Indian Movement and the Panthers seemed to confirm our analysis. Both movements were crushed by the authorities, also because they simply didn't have the support that would have been needed to withstand the attacks.

Can you tell us more about Greenland? What was your analysis?

Jan: The analysis of Greenland wasn't a high priority, because the territory had no real significance on the global level. But there was in particular one KUF member who addressed the question in a few articles in *Ungkommunisten*, mainly to draw attention to the fact that Denmark was a colonial power, too.

*The Weather Underground also had a clearly anti-imperialist program.
In their book* Prairie Fire: The Politics of Revolutionary Anti-Imperialism *they stated that "Third World Liberation is leading the struggle against imperialism."[15] Yet it seems you shared the critique formulated by the LSM member Carroll Ishee in his "Critical Remarks on Prairie Fire."[16]*

Torkil: Carroll Ishee's critique is comradely and expresses respect for the Weather Underground's internationalist perspective and practice. He sees the LSM and the WU agreeing in the central revolutionary force of the time being the oppressed nations and liberation movements. His critique focuses on the Weather Underground having illusions about the possible support of Third World liberation struggles by the U.S. working class. He did not share the idea of the Weather Underground that militant actions could have a radicalizing effect on the working class. The LSM did in no way reject armed struggle in the metropole, but such a struggle had to be coordinated with the anti-imperialist struggle in the Third World. For example, some Weather Underground actions such as the bombing of the Pentagon in May 1972

---

15. *Prairie Fire* was originally "printed underground in the U.S. for the people" in 1974 and distributed by the "Prairie Fire Distributing Committee."

16. *LSM News* 1, no. 2, Summer 1975.

or of Gulf Oil in June 1974 had positive effects in putting the focus on the struggle in the Third World, but they could have been far more effective had they been linked directly and concretely to Third World struggles, rather than mainly remaining on a symbolic level. As an exemplary action, Ishee mentions the attack on the army headquarters in Lisbon by the Portuguese Revolutionary Brigades in April 1973: the brigades took many valuable documents with them and sent copies to the liberation movements in Portugal's African colonies.[17]

In many ways, the LSM's critique of the WU resembles our critique of the RAF. We also saw them as comrades and supported their actions against imperialism and its institutions. But we felt they had a wrong analysis of the political and economic conditions and therefore a wrong revolutionary perspective.

Jan: However, one has to say that the activities of the Weather Underground certainly made the imperialist war in Southeast Asia more difficult to fight, and that already means a lot.

Carroll Ishee, the LSM member penning the "Critical Remarks on Prairie Fire," died in 1981, when he was fighting with the FMLN in El Salvador. Did you ever consider joining a liberation movement?

Jan: There were discussions about that in Denmark in the late 1960s. Some folks were quite serious about it. There was a group called "Volunteers for Vietnam."[18] Holger was somewhat involved with them. They were ready to go fight with the Viet Cong and traveled to the Vietnamese embassy in Prague to present themselves. However, the ambassador basically asked them, very politely, to go home. Some of them took that hard. But of course the ambassador was right. How are ten youths from Denmark going to help the Viet Cong in the jungle? They don't know the environment, they are unfamiliar with the culture, they can't speak the language. When they're finally down with malaria, they are nothing but a burden. For us, it was more important to

---

17. The Portuguese Brigadas Revolucionárias were a militant left-wing group active in the early 1970s.

18. In Danish, *Forening af Vietnamfrivillige*.

build a strong organization in the metropole, where we were based, in order to provide useful support. We discussed many forms of support, but the conclusion always was that providing money and other material supplies was most useful.

Torkil: When you are twenty years old, it is easy to see yourself as a heroic freedom fighter in the Third World. But those glorious images quickly fade once you really see the reality of the liberation struggle. Besides, the more we got to know about liberation movements, the more we also got to understand that there was no lack of manpower. In the 1970s, millions of people were ready to die for socialism. There were many Europeans ready to join the PFLP. That's why providing money seemed more useful to us. And I'm sure for the liberation movements, too. They wanted ten million crowns more than a few extra fighters. The only exceptions were people with special skills. Marc Rudin, for example, played an important role for the PFLP because he knew a lot about graphics and radio communication.

As for Carroll Ishee and the FMLN, I don't know the details of that story. According to the rebel radio *Venceremos*, his final words were: "Tell my wife, my daughter, and my American people that I have died fulfilling my duties." He obviously had strong convictions.

PFLP Bulletin, September 1981;
Cover art by Marc Rudin.

The following quote is from the article "Can White ~~Workers~~ Radicals Be Radicalized?" written in the late 1960s by Ted Allen,[19] who later got widespread recognition for his two-volume work The Invention of the White Race.[20] *It's a critique of a position that sounds close to yours. Allen says that the "Artful-dodge No. 5" is one of the common strategies to defend the position. How would you respond to the critique?*

Artful-dodge No. 5:

(The most "radical" sounding) "Don't waste time on the United States white workers. For the time being, forget them. The privileges of these workers are paid for by the super-profits wrung out of the super-exploited black, yellow and brown labor of colonial peoples (including the special case of the oppressed Negro in the United States). The victorious national liberation struggles of these peoples will, sooner or later, chop off these sources of white-skin privilege funds. Then, though not before, the white workers will 'get the message.' Meantime, the role of white radicals is simply to 'support' the colonial liberation struggles."

This is 1) wrong; 2) dishonest; 3) cowardly.

Wrong, because it confuses the white-skin privilege in general, which is the prerogative of every white person living in the United States, with the special form of that privilege, the payment (direct or indirect) to the "aristocracy" of labor above what would be necessary according to the laws of normal competition, and which enables those few workers to escape in all but a formal sense from the proletarian to the petit-bourgeois life... .

Dishonest, because it promises to "support" the black struggle, but refuses to give the most meaningful "support" of all, i.e., to

---

19. The article was included in the pamphlet *White Blindspot & Can White ~~Workers~~ Radicals Be Radicalized?* (1969), authored by Noel Ignatin [Ignatiev] and Ted Allen, and published by the SDS's Radical Education Project.

20. Theodore W. Allen, *The Invention of the White Race,* 2 vols. (New York: Verso, 1994/1997).

challenge the ideology and practice of white supremacy among the white workers.

Cowardly, because it chooses the role of "supply troops" rather than that of "front-line fighters" against the vile racist theory and practice of white supremacy.

Torkil: Allen presents the position he is criticizing in very moralistic and voluntaristic terms. This was not our approach. We were much more structural. Well, maybe in the late 1960s we held positions close to the one criticized here. At that time, we did use terms like "bribery" to describe the relationship between the capitalist class and the working class. But from a Marxist perspective, that was the wrong approach. The problem is not that anyone is consciously led astray, the problem is that the material conditions create specific economic interests and forms of consciousness, which in turn lead to specific forms of social relationships and institutions. So, white workers were not "evil" or "guilty," it was simply not in their interest to radically change the global economic order.

Regarding the statement being "wrong": in a formal sense, the labor aristocracy has nothing to do with skin color but with wages and living standards. At the same time, racism of course played a crucial role in the U.S. in the 1960s, when the civil rights movement was at its height. In our analysis, poor Americans were not considered part of the labor aristocracy as a whole. But most white workers were.

Regarding the statement being "dishonest": I don't think that applied to us. Over a twenty-year period, we were very open about our ideas and experienced strong rejection from other leftist organizations because of it. We were very clear about challenging the ideology of the labor aristocracy.

Regarding the statement being "cowardly": All people have limits in terms of how far they can go, and I think these limits need to be respected. This was always the guideline within our organization.

Jan: Discussions about white supremacy weren't prevalent in Europe at the time. The quote strongly reflects an American context, and, as we stated before, there were some significant differences. I do, however, recall discussions about settler culture, which were relevant for most liberation movements, as they were all facing similar patterns: settlers had arrived as self-appointed carriers of civilization with a supposedly higher culture and superior means of production, treating indigenous people as subhuman. This was the case in Algeria as much as in South Africa and elsewhere. Now, in the context of the U.S., with the oppression of the indigenous population and the slave trade, the history of European settlement left a strong legacy with long-term negative effects for American culture, including working-class culture. I understand that the questions raised in Allen's quote had a particular relevance in that context.

Anti-imperialist Practice and M-KA

You have already mentioned a common critique of the First World anti-imperialist movements of the 1970s and 1980s, namely that they romanticized Third World liberation struggles. How do you respond to this?

Torkil: Well, if there was a problem with leftist romanticization at the time, it was the romanticization of the Western working class. I don't think that we can be accused of romanticizing anything. I think we were very realistic. Once you were in close contact with liberation movements, there was little space for romanticization. The cynicism of realpolitik was very tangible, and you were constantly forced to compromise. We certainly did not live under the illusion that we were working with saints.

What were some of the compromises you had to make?

Jan: The most obvious was that we couldn't stand behind every single action of the movements we supported. If we take the PFLP, for example, there were many actions that we found problematic. Without taking any moral high ground, we really weren't happy about their collaboration with the Japanese Red Army[21] or with the relations they had to the governments that protected

---

21. The Japanese Red Army was founded as a militant Marxist and anti-imperialist group in 1971. It was most notorious for a 1971 attack at Tel Aviv's airport that left twenty-eight people dead, the majority Christian pilgrims from Puerto Rico.

them. Of course there are "good" and "bad" anti-imperialist actions, even if the boundaries aren't always that clear.

Torkil: One problem is that it is easy to be idealistic and principled in theory and very easy to judge the actions of others. But once you act yourself, it is very hard not to make your hands dirty.

Jan: We must also remember that spectacular actions were important for organizations to raise attention and attract members. Various Palestinian groups were vying for supporters at the time and there was fierce competition. This led some to engage in actions that did not necessarily fit their political line. That was not only the case for the PFLP, but also for the DFLP. On the one hand, they tried to establish a broad grassroots movement, including sections of the Israeli left. On the other hand, they engaged in actions that got them attention but didn't necessarily correspond to their political goals.

You regularly used the slogan, "Solidarity is something you can hold in your hands." Where did it originate from?

Torkil: We used the slogan with regard to the majority of anti-imperialist groups in Europe. There was a strong focus on solidarity demonstrations and petitions and the like. They called it "political solidarity." We just wanted to make it clear that this wasn't enough. What really counted was material support. And I think the message is still important. Just recently, I read a new PhD thesis on international solidarity work in Denmark in the 1970s, and Tøj til Afrika and Ulandskluserne aren't even mentioned. I think this is very telling.

Jan: Expressing solidarity is nice. But if it never translates into anything concrete, its powers are limited. For us, the expression of solidarity was nothing but a first step. As Torkil says, the decisive thing was to provide actual, tangible support.

At the same time I read that you, Jan, never saw your activities as an "alternative to the Red Cross"—what did you mean by that?

Jan: The Red Cross relieves pain and suffering. Our intention was to help change the political and economic structures that cause pain and suffering.

A former member of your group has suggested that you might have been able to provide more support if you had stuck to legal activities. What do you make of that?

Jan: Well, the facts are very clear. The maximum amount of money we were able to raise legally in a year was about half a million crowns—and this required the very dedicated and time-consuming work of dozens of people. This didn't even compare to what we could make illegally. I really can't see how we could have secured the funds we did with legal means.

There has been much speculation about whether Gotfred Appel knew about the illegal activities of KAK members during the 1970s. Can you comment on that?

Jan: Did he know about them? He planned everything! KAK was a very hierarchical organization. Everything, down to the tiniest detail, was decided by the leadership. At the time the illegal practice began, the leadership consisted of Gotfred, Ulla, and Holger—with Gotfred being at the center of it all.

Did the money you made in the 1970s go exclusively to liberation movements, or was some used for KAK's infrastructure?

Jan: For the most part, the money went to liberation movements. After all, that was the motivation behind the illegal activities. KAK could be maintained by legal means, not least because all members donated 10 to 30 percent of their income. In M-KA, a small part of the money acquired illegally was used for rent, travels, etc. But most of the organization's costs were covered by member contributions.

You have already stressed that KAK was a very disciplined organization. Did that help with the criminal activities? You ended up becoming Denmark's most successful twentieth-century robbers.

Jan: Discipline is important for building a strong organization, and it is important for effective illegal work. We learned early on from practical experience that a lack of discipline could mean less money, to put it bluntly. So, in that sense, there was a connection. At the same time, I would say that other factors were at least as important. For me personally, two things were crucial. First, a strong commitment to the organization: we had promised each other to make a difference, and I wanted to do my part. Second, an acknowledgment of the faith that the organization put into you: you were selected for a certain task and you didn't want to let the organization down. It was the shared political goal that was decisive. Outside coercion or pressure were not needed. At least not in my case. Others might have felt differently.

Among the robberies you have been accused of one stands out, as the methods don't fit in with the others ascribed to you. In 1980, some men tricked their way into the home of a bank manager in the Copenhagen suburb of Glostrup and held family members hostage while forcing the manager to accompany them to the bank in order to open the safe. Can you comment on this?

Jan: After we had been arrested, the police included this unresolved case in the list of crimes they wanted to charge us for. Since there was no evidence at all, the charges were dropped. It speaks to Øvig Knudsen's fondness for conspiracy theories that he included the story in his book nonetheless. However, we had nothing to do with it; it ain't more complicated than that.

KAK was dissolved in 1978 after the so-called anti–gender discrimination campaign. The organization split into three groups …

Jan: Well, but that took two steps. First, Gotfred and Ulla basically removed themselves by not acknowledging their mistakes and by trying to use their authority to keep KAK under their control. Then, there was the split between M-KA and MAG. The most important difference between M-KA and MAG was that the folks involved in MAG questioned everything: our political line, our organizational structure, our practice, both the legal and the illegal part, and so on. They suggested exclusively focusing on studies for some time in order to find a new direction. We in M-KA agreed that changes were necessary, but we wanted to resume our activities as quickly as possible and make adjustments along the way. We just saw our activities as too important to put them on hold.

Did the decision to continue the illegal work come easily?

Torkil: Yes. We felt that we had an obligation towards the movements we collaborated with. We couldn't justify being idle. That was the main reason for M-KA choosing a different path than other former KAK members.

Why did the PFLP trust you after the KAK split and not Gotfred Appel?

Jan: The PFLP understood quickly that our group was the only one that could continue the illegal practice. We had the experience and the means. Our relationship with Gotfred and Ulla was complicated after KAK's breakup. They were living in a house that was in Holger's name. We gave them three months' notice to move out, but they refused. We also weren't sure whether they would mention our activities to others. Since it was clearly in the PFLP's interest that the illegal practice continued, they were happy to send someone to talk to Gotfred and Ulla when we asked them. Gotfred and Ulla were told that Holger had become a PFLP member and that he was under the direct protection of the organization from then on. That wasn't true, but it was a tactical move to ensure that Gotfred and Ulla wouldn't make things difficult for us. It worked. They moved out of the house and we never heard from them again.

How would you summarize the biggest differences between KAK and M-KA?

Torkil: Gotfred Appel was a charismatic and bright theorist and Ulla Hauton a rigid leader. One of the problems of KAK was that there was no room for individual initiative. People only acted upon orders; anything else would have been "undisciplined." This meant that a lot of potential, based on individual knowledge, skill, and motivation, remained unused. Once Gotfred and Ulla were out of the picture, there was a possibility for a horizontal organizational structure and a division of labor and tasks. That's what characterized M-KA, even if informal leadership existed.

Another important factor was that M-KA offered the possibility for theoretical development. In KAK, the theoretical body was limited to Marx, Engels, Lenin, Mao, and Gotfred Appel himself. In my eyes, the theory hadn't developed at all since it was first formulated in the late 1960s.

Jan: I agree that the changes were overall positive. We became less dogmatic and prejudiced, and we enriched our theory by adding Arghiri Emmanuel's analysis of unequal exchange. But we also encountered some challenges that we had no proper answers to. Perhaps most significantly, our circle of supporters and sympathizers decreased steadily. Partly, this might have been a consequence of general political developments, that is, of anti-imperialism becoming weaker. But we also had ourselves to blame.

Torkil: That is true. We had difficulties mobilizing sympathizers. However, I think the problem dates back all the way to 1972, when KAK developed the illegal practice. Security was ever more important and it became difficult to integrate new members. Plus, it was clear that we would never gain mass support with our political ideas—they simply weren't very popular in our part of the world.

In "It Is All About Politics" you write that for Gotfred Appel "support for Third World liberation movements had a clear Danish perspective," while for M-KA "supporting liberation movements was a revolutionary end in itself." At the same time, you still claimed in the 1980s that "the emancipation of the proletariat in the exploited countries is a precondition for the destruction of the imperialist system and the introduction of socialism in Denmark."[22] This doesn't sound so different from Appel's position.

---

22. From the chapter "What Can Communists in the Imperialist Countries Do?" in the M-KA book *Unequal Exchange and the Prospects of Socialism*, published in 1986 (Danish original, *Imperialismen idag: Det ulige bytte og mulighederne för socialisme i en delt verden* [Imperialism Today: Unequal Exchange and the Possibilities for Socialism in a Divided World], 1983).

Jan: We aren't talking about a complete shift in our politics. But M-KA definitely focused less on the development of socialism in Denmark than KAK did. We still believed that successful socialist movements in the Third World would strengthen socialism in the imperialist countries, but we didn't believe that this would happen anytime soon. It was nothing that we could influence in the here and now. So the focus on the support of the liberation movements became even stronger than it had been in KAK. That's what we mean when we say that it was an end in itself—it was more than just an instrument for introducing socialism in Denmark. Perhaps the differences with KAK's position were gradual, but they clearly existed.

You write in "It Is All About Politics" that M-KA had a "democratically elected leadership." What exactly did that mean?

Torkil: The leadership of M-KA consisted of three to four people who were appointed in an informal process based on consensus. They coordinated everything, so that different activities wouldn't clash with one another: the legal and illegal practice, theoretical studies, the publishing work, etc. They also called for meetings, paid the bills, and took care of other administrative tasks. About every other month, the whole group—about fifteen people— had a full-day meeting, where important decisions were made, also based on consensus.

You mentioned Arghiri Emmanuel: I read that in the 1970s he calculated that if the world's wealth was distributed equally, everyone could afford the living standard of an average Portuguese. Apparently, you took this as a guideline for how to live your own lives. Is that true?

Jan: No. In KAK, the political and the private were clearly divided. No one had a moral investment in how others lived their lives. This was also true for M-KA, although the political and the private overlapped a bit more. There was overall a stronger social dimension in M-KA.

Torkil: In general, members lived simple but normal lives. Some, like myself, chose to be unemployed for years. If you were unemployed long-term, you received 80 percent of the minimum wage. That was enough for a comfortable life.

In the documentary film Blekingegadebanden, *a former PET agent recalls listening to a bugged telephone conversation between Torkil and Lisa. Torkil said that he needed some dental work done but couldn't afford it. This was a few weeks after the Købmagergade robbery. Did you never use any of the funds from your robberies for personal matters?*

Jan: The money we got through the illegal practice was one thing. Our personal finances were another. In certain cases, there might have been an overlap. For example, it was necessary for each of us to have a car; mainly for security reasons, since we often were under observation. One time, Niels needed a new car but had no money, so he got a few thousand crowns to buy an old used one. But in general, personal finances were kept completely separate from the group's. At times, we had bags with thousands of crowns in cash, since we always kept some for upcoming actions. Whenever someone took money from the bag, he left a note with the amount and what it was needed for. This might sound pedantic, but such routines were very important for the kind of work we did.

What was the relationship between Tøj til Afrika and M-KA like? Was it different to the one between TTA and KAK?

Jan: I don't think there was a big difference. The main one was that in M-KA, TTA members were more integrated into the political discussions. In KAK, they mainly were subjects of what we called "political schooling."

Torkil: Between KAK and TTA members, there had been a clear hierarchy. This was not as pronounced in M-KA. But in general, TTA remained a doorway into the political organization. That was the same in relation to both KAK and M-KA.

What was the TTA membership like in the 1980s compared to the 1970s?

Torkil: Numbers dropped perhaps a little, but not much. I would say there were about twenty folks in Copenhagen and ten each in Odense and Århus.

Why did TTA disband in 1986?

Jan: There were several reasons. First of all, TTA focused on sending clothes, shoes, and tents to refugee camps administered by African liberation movements. During the 1980s, these camps disappeared. A SWAPO-administered camp in Angola was the last big one we supported. In general, new means of support were needed. Simultaneously, it became more difficult to collect things in Denmark. During the 1980s, a whole new culture of selling used things developed and people now often tried to make money off of them rather than giving them away. Finally, we had been doing this for a long time and were simply looking for something new.

That's why you opened Café Liberation in 1987. I was wondering what the clientele was like, especially since you weren't that popular among the Danish left.

Torkil: The clients were just regular folks. It wasn't a particularly political crowd, although we organized some political events in the café.

How did it go financially?

Jan: Unfortunately, we didn't make much money. I think we were just a bit ahead of our time, to be honest. These days, places like Café Liberation— what we call "café latte places" in Denmark—have become very popular. Back then, this was a new concept. Hip urban coffee shop culture wasn't born yet. We would have made more money with a traditional pub.

Once you were arrested, the café was forced to close down, is that right?

Torkil: Yes, under the circumstances it was impossible to keep it open. But the remaining volunteers closed it down in a very responsible manner. All of the remaining funds went to different social movements.

In the press, Jan has often been called the "leader" of the Blekingegade Group and Torkil the "chief ideologue." Is there any truth to these characterizations?

Torkil: I would put it this way: Jan had been involved for a long time and he was the most experienced of us. So, naturally, his opinion was respected. As for my role as a "chief ideologue," I wrote the drafts for many position papers and articles, but I always got feedback from the entire group before finishing them.

Jan: I think these labels mainly exist to satisfy the needs of categorization that the police and the media have. The police probably also thought that there was truth to them, because they relied on Gotfred Appel's outdated knowledge about us.[23] They knew that I had been part of KAK's leadership and drew their conclusions. Torkil was very engaged in theoretical studies and, as he says, drafted many of our texts. In that sense, he was probably more of a "chief ideologue" than I was a "leader."

During your trial it became known that you had been under PET observation for a long time. Were you surprised that you hadn't been arrested earlier?

Jan: We knew that we had been under on-and-off surveillance for many years. I always figured that PET simply tried to gather as much information about our group as possible. When we were observed, we never engaged in anything illegal. Then, when the observation ended, normality returned, and we continued with our practice.

One can wonder, of course, why PET never even tried to give us a fright. They could have arrested us or called us in for questioning at any time. This might not have gotten us convicted, but would we have had the spirit to continue with the illegal practice afterward? I'm not sure.

Especially after the Lyngby robbery, when two PFLP members were arrested in Paris with six million Danish crowns, it was strange that PET wasn't more active. This would have been a perfect opportunity to put us in a bad spot. I don't know why this didn't happen.

---

23. After the arrest of the Blekingegade Group members in April 1989, Gotfred Appel was questioned by the police about the group's background.

To this day, I wonder what PET really thought of us. They clearly suspected us of something, but how much did they really know? There are only two possibilities, and neither sheds a good light on PET: the first one is that we were indeed the main suspects in some robberies, but that PET didn't have much interest in that and was more interested in catching bigger fish, namely PFLP members, perhaps also considering their collaboration with the Mossad; the other possibility is that, despite the frequent observation and other efforts, they simply didn't have a clue.

The Danish government has summoned several investigative commissions to shed light on the role that PET played over the years, albeit with few relevant findings. This has not ended the controversy. In 2009, the chief investigator in the criminal case against you, Jørn Moos, criticized PET harshly in the book Politiets hemmeligheder.[24] *Not least because of this, another investigative commission was convened in 2010, with a report expected for 2014.[25] Do you think anything will come of it this time?*

Torkil: You never know, but I don't expect much. As you say, there have already been several investigations, and PET always managed to disclose very little. I can't see why it would be different this time around.

Jan, there have been claims that you had access to police files because of your work at Regnecentralen, the IT company.

Jan: This has been exaggerated. I didn't have access to police files. But it is true that our company installed a search engine for a computer system used by the police, which gave me—and also my brother Bo, who worked at the same company—insight into some of their data. I can see the irony in that, but the data we had access to never proved very useful.

On two occasions, members of your group were arrested by the police: Peter Døllner in 1981 because of using a fake ID at a post office, and Niels

---

24. For publications regarding Jørn Moos, see the introduction.

25. The official website of the commission is http://www. blekingegadekommissionen.dk (in Danish).

Jørgensen in 1986 after a failed car theft. Did that cause great concern for you?

Torkil: Of course we were aware that these incidents could cause problems for us, but both passed without any bigger consequences. Peter used a fake ID to collect some money for a car we had sold. He was detained for a few days, but nothing much came of it.

The case with Niels was a little trickier. In general, car theft wasn't a big deal, cars were stolen all the time in Copenhagen. The bigger problem was that Niels carried a bunch of things that a regular car thief wouldn't carry, such as a walkie-talkie, a professional tool set, stuff like that. Still, he was released after just one day and the whole thing was treated as an ordinary affair and settled with a fine. Niels was never asked any questions that could have compromised us. A year and a half later, though, he was called in for questioning. He went to his lawyer, who talked to the police and explained to them that the case had been closed for six months. Niels never heard anything again. The only possible explanation is that PET got to know about the incident half a year too late and clumsily tried to revive the case.

In the beginning, we also were nervous when we were under observation. We didn't know whether this meant that we'd be arrested soon. But once you've experienced this several times, you become more relaxed. Whenever more of us were observed at the same time, we made sure that at least one of us disappeared and hid in a secret apartment, until the danger was over. This was to prevent all of us being arrested at once. We should have followed this routine in April 1989, but we had become tired over the years and negligent with security. I guess we assumed that, as usual, the observation would eventually just end.

In "It Is All About Politics" you write that it was a series of small mistakes that eventually led to your arrest. What kind of mistakes?

Torkil: Mainly careless communication with liberation movements—even if their European representatives were to blame in many ways. Their security standards often differed from ours. But there were other mistakes, too. For example, we regularly used the same methods for stealing cars, the same types of fake documents, etc. We were aware of the problem and tried to use as many variations as possible, and we also planted false evidence to deter the police. But in the end, the way we operated tied our robberies together. Still, it took the police nearly twenty years to connect the dots.

I assume it was no coincidence that your arrest finally came after a policeman was killed.

Torkil: We knew that the search would be particularly intense. But we hadn't left any traces and felt safe—probably a bit too safe.

Jan: When I read that the Copenhagen police department, the federal police, and PET had created a joint investigative team, I got worried. I figured that this could only mean that we were the main suspects. Why else would PET be involved? We did, in fact, discuss improving security, but, as Torkil has said, we were all a bit tired and extra security measures would have meant compromises for both our political and private life. Apparently, we weren't willing to make those. But the single biggest mistake was not even following our usual security standards.

An obvious question is why so many incriminating notes regarding the Købmagergade robbery were left at the Blekingegade apartment.

Jan: Yes, that is an obvious question. We knew that we were under observation for some time after the robbery, so we didn't want to clean out the apartment then. And afterward, things just got delayed. Having said that, we probably wouldn't have gotten rid of all the incriminating material anyway. The truck we robbed hadn't just carried cash but also other valuables, for example a precious stamp collection. I assume we would have kept those things in order to turn them into money later. To be honest, under the circumstances it might have been an advantage for us that the evidence regarding the Købmagergade robbery was so strong. Having such clear evidence on one action meant that it became the focus of the prosecution. It is not surprising that we got acquitted on most other counts.

Do you think you might have never gone to prison had the police not found the keys?

Jan: Yes, that's a reality we have to live with. Without the keys, I don't think there would have been a trial. Before the apartment was found, the police had no solid evidence at all—none. Furthermore, if they hadn't found the keys on us, we could have reacted differently to our arrest. We could have complained about the "unjustified persecution of left-wing activists" and so on. But since we had to avoid any questions regarding the keys, we could only keep our mouths shut and wait.

If the apartment hadn't been found and you had been released, what would have happened?

Jan: One or two men would have gone underground and cleared out the apartment. Going underground for a week or two wouldn't have been a problem. We knew places in Copenhagen where you could shake off anyone following you within a few seconds, you just needed to be a few steps ahead. After clearing out the apartment, we would have had two options: finding a new apartment or ending the illegal practice. But we never got to that point.

The Z-File

A particularly controversial aspect of your work was the so-called "Z-file," the "Z" standing for "Zionism." Can you explain the background?

Jan: In principle, we were offering liberation movements the support they needed. Usually, it came down to material support, but we had experiences with other activities, too, including the collection of data, observation, and so forth. So, at one point we were approached by the PFLP who wanted us to help uncover Israeli agents in Denmark. The PFLP leadership had become increasingly worried about the high number of "leftist European tourists" passing through the Middle East, who often got a good idea of the PFLP's infrastructure.

Torkil: One also has to consider the Danish context. PET had been observing the Palestinian community in Denmark since the early 1970s and it collaborated closely with the Mossad. This is not a vague suspicion, there is plenty of documentation for it. It became obvious during our trial that information resulting from the observation of Palestinians in Denmark landed on the Mossad's desk—in English. Ole Stig Andersen, the chief of PET from 1975 to 1984, also writes extensively about the collaboration in his memoirs.[26] And then there was the Wejra scandal, which disclosed connections between the Danish weapons industry and Israel.[27] In short, Denmark was very important for the Mossad in the 1970s and '80s. The PFLP asking us to help with uncovering Israeli agents was related to this.

How did you proceed?

Jan: At first, we were skeptical, because it was work that required much time and energy, while we wanted to focus on our own actions. But Bo had recently joined M-KA, and he had the skills, the time, and the will to do it—and so he went to work. Torkil and I took on the role of advisers, based on our own experiences: people who get involved in illegal political activities have often been very public about their beliefs but then they suddenly disappear. Of course it is possible that they simply lost interest in politics, but it is also possible that they started doing things they don't want the public to know about. So, based on this assumption, we were looking for pro-Israeli activists who had suddenly disappeared. Bo created two categories, one for companies, organizations, and journals supporting Israel, and one for individuals. In the end, the file contained many Jews, also because we thought that it'd be most likely for the Mossad to recruit in the Jewish community. But it was never a "Jew file," as reported by several media outlets.

Was the information ever put to use?

Jan: Not really. There was one person we considered a possible agent, but confirming that would have required time and effort—round-the-clock observation, wiretapping, etc.—that we weren't able to commit to this, even

---

26. Ole Stig Andersen, *En PET-Chefs erindringer* [The Memoirs of a PET Chief] (Copenhagen: Sohn, 2012).

27. See p. 73 n. 47.

though we had the equipment. In the end, there wasn't much more than the file itself, with copies going to the PFLP. If those copies ever were of any use to them, I don't know. It's not very likely, though. To be honest, the whole thing wasn't very professional and it had never been a priority for us. I mean, let's say we had really succeeded in uncovering an Israeli agent—then what? We certainly didn't want to end up in a clinch with the Mossad. But we never even thought that far when we started compiling the information. We just wanted to do the PFLP a favor. Their desire to keep spies disguised as left-wing tourists away from their infrastructure was very reasonable.

From what I understand, the public reaction was very strong when the file was discovered in the Blekingegade apartment.

Jan: Yes, the press dubbed it the "Jew file" and we were accused of being anti-Semites. The police also informed everyone who was named in it, which caused much distress; people were wondering whether they were on a hit list.

So, in the end, the file did little more than instill fear in people?

Jan: The file was foolish, we don't have to discuss this. I mean, there was nothing wrong with looking at the Mossad's activities in Denmark, but listing individuals in that manner made no sense. As I said, the whole thing wasn't very well thought through; it was ill-prepared.

Torkil: Especially in light of today's growing racism and anti-Semitism, we very much regret the way the file was put together. It is very discomforting to know that some people believed they had landed on a blacklist because of their religious or ethnic background. That was never the intention.

Did the Z-file also cause strong reactions within the Danish left?

Jan: No, that wasn't my impression. It was mainly the mainstream media that picked up on it.

Torkil: The Danish left strongly distinguishes between anti-Zionism and anti-Semitism. In the late 1960s, this was still different. Back then, the Danish left was very supportive of Israel and we were accused of being anti-Semites when handing out leaflets in support of the Palestinian struggle. Things started to change after the 1973 war, and then there was a very strong shift in perspective after the Sabra and Shatila massacres in 1982.[28] There was strong coverage of the events in the Danish media, which had a big impact on the country. The Intifada and the pictures of Israeli soldiers mistreating Palestinian children also played an important role.

Jan: A big problem is that the boundaries between anti-Zionism and anti-Semitism have often been blurred. This usually happens to discredit the Palestinian resistance, but certain actions of Palestinian groups have also contributed to this. If we take the example of the *Achille Lauro* hijacking in 1985, when the commando executed an elderly, wheelchair-bound Jew, we have a perfect example.[29] Such actions are simply disastrous. Given the circumstances of the conflict, there have always been anti-Semitic sentiments in Palestinian organizations, including in the PFLP's rank and file. But the official line of the PFLP was very clear on the issue and there was absolutely no room for anti-Semitism.

However, especially in the German-speaking left, many would argue that the Z-file and the impact it had on Denmark's Jewish community was but a logical consequence of anti-Zionist and anti-imperialist politics, proving that, at their core, they are anti-Semitic ideologies.

Jan: I understand that, but of course I can't agree with it.

---

28. See p. 68 n. 45.

29. In October 1985, the cruise ship *Achille Lauro* was hijacked off the Egyptian shore by a commando of the Palestine Liberation Front (PFL), a splinter group of the PFLP-GC (see the appendix). The seventy-nine-year-old Leon Klinghoffer was shot dead after the ship was refused permission to enter the Syrian port of Tartus. Being promised safe conduct, the PFL commando later surrendered in Egypt without its demands of having fifty Palestinian prisoners released from Israeli prisons being met.

Torkil: It is also very difficult for us to relate to these arguments on a personal level. Jan's parents were active in the resistance against the Nazis, and my wife's Jewish family had to flee to Sweden during the war in order to avoid deportation to a German concentration camp. We abhor anti-Semitism. Besides, fighting anti-Semitism is an important part of the anti-Zionist struggle; after all, anti-Semitism is the root cause of the Israeli settler state.

In Prison

After your arrest, you refused to be labeled as "political prisoners." Why?

Torkil: Basically, because there was nothing political about our actions themselves, especially not in the context of Danish society. We didn't attack the Danish state or any of it institutions or representatives. We used criminal methods to acquire material means for Third World liberation movements. So, within the Danish context, we were nothing but common criminals. We never sent out communiqués to explain our actions. That wasn't our strategy, and we didn't pretend anything different once we were arrested. For twenty years, we did everything we could to make our actions look like common crimes. If you do that, then you can't just stand there and yell, "But it was all political, let me to go free!" once you face time in prison. That would be ridiculous. Of course, our intentions were political, but that's a different thing. If anyone needs a label, I guess we were "politically motivated criminals."

Jan: You become a political prisoner in the context of a political struggle. We weren't involved in any political struggle in Denmark. Had we been caught in Israel or in Lebanon, things might have been different. It also made perfect sense that the urban guerrilla comrades in Germany claimed the status of political prisoners. They were engaged in an open conflict with the German state. We were just robbing cash-in-transit trucks.

At the same time, in "It Is All About Politics," you justify your methods by claiming that you were part of an international struggle. Did you consider this morally relevant, but not legally?

Torkil: The boundaries here aren't clear. You can see things in a national context and in an international one. Which perspective you prioritize depends on the situation. Morally, the international perspective was very important to us, because we were internationalists and our criminal activities were motivated by the desire to support liberation movements in the Third World. Legally, we had to relate to the Danish context, because that was where we lived, where we were active, and where we were arrested and sentenced. But even that depends on the situation. At the time, the fact that our robberies were motivated by wanting to support the PFLP and other organizations was legally irrelevant. It was not possible to indict us for terrorism, because the Danish laws weren't written that way. Today, this has changed. Recently, Anton Nielsen, the seventy-two-year-old chairman of the Horserød-Stutthof Foreningen, an antifascist organization founded by Danes who fought against the fascist European regimes in the 1930s and '40s, was sentenced to two months in prison because his organization had collected money for the PFLP. A couple of weeks ago, he began serving his time in the Horserød State Prison—the same prison his father was at in 1941 before being transferred to the Stutthof Concentration Camp. Now, if we had been in a similar position and gotten extra prison time because of our support for liberation movements, we might have very well called ourselves political prisoners. All of this really depends on the circumstances.

Jan: The basic moral questions remain the same, of course. We have tried to discuss them from various angles in "It Is All About Politics" and there is no need to repeat ourselves here. But I can illustrate the key difficulties with a couple of questions: Was it right that the Danish resistance movement executed alleged informants during World War II? If you answer that question positively, you have to understand that things can go wrong and that innocent people might get hurt. If you answer it negatively, you might retain your moral purity, but you also have to accept that some people will be tortured and killed because informants weren't stopped. Was it right for the Wollweber League to blow up ships that Franco's troops would have used to fight the republican forces?[30] If you say yes, you have to live with the fact that

---

30. Regarding the Wollweber League, see "It Is All About Politics."

the bombs can hurt or even kill civilians. If you say no, then what about the people who would have been killed with the help of these ships?

The problems in the world aren't black and white. If you get involved in conflict, it is hard to keep your hands clean, even if you fight on the side of the oppressed. Today, certain forms of civil disobedience and extraparliamentary action are morally accepted. The criminal means we used are not. It is up to each and any individual to judge them. Personally, I sleep well at night knowing what I have done.

I understand that you were also politically active as prisoners. Can you tell us about that? Were all imprisoned members of the Blekingegade Group politically active in prison?

Torkil: Yes, more or less. Niels and I were spokespeople for the prisoners in our respective wards, and Jan was the editor of the prisoners' magazine.

Jan: If you were a political prisoner—as, for example the comrades in Germany were—your political struggle continued in prison. We, on the other hand, went into prison under the same conditions as anybody else. This was the basis we could organize on: not as a separate group, but as a part of the overall prison population. We approached this as communists. We tried to prove to other prisoners that they could achieve more if they were united. Prison culture often builds on individual acts of violence and intimidation. That's the usual way of achieving things. We tried to demonstrate that collective action was more effective. It wasn't easy, but we had some success.

For example?

Torkil: One fairly successful campaign concerned the heroin trade in prison, which caused many conflicts among the inmates. We were not against the dealing of soft drugs or against bringing heroin into prison for personal use. But we regarded the heroin trade as very damaging to the prisoners' community, and so did many others, which is why we managed to get a lot of support and reduce the trade significantly. We also had success with campaigns against special units for what you call "negative" prisoners in Denmark: prisoners who do not cooperate with the authorities and are

Prisoners' journal *Brasen* (Danish slang for "prison"),
editor Jan Weimann, cover art Marc Rudin.

considered a bad influence on other inmates. Furthermore, we started a campaign against the particularly harsh treatment of Marc Rudin in Horsens State Prison. He was held in isolation almost the entire time and always had to deal with special restrictions. The argument was that he was a particular flight risk.

Jan: It was important to find issues that many prisoners could rally around. For example, we got plenty of support when we brought attention to the situation of Palle Sørensen, a convicted police murderer. Palle had killed four policemen in 1965, and he was still in prison when we got there twenty-five years later. In Denmark, that's a very long time. So in 1990, on the twenty-fifth anniversary of his sentencing, we started a "Free Palle" campaign. Other prisoners knew that if you killed four children you got out after sixteen years, so why should you be locked up forever for killing four cops? There was a widely shared sentiment among the prison population that this was unjust.

Another example concerned a vendor who had a monopoly on selling foodstuffs and other necessities in prison. He charged very high prices. We organized a boycott and he was replaced by a vendor whose prices were much lower. It was a simple but effective means of collective action.

Torkil: Resistance is crucial in the prison environment. We are talking about an extremely controlled space. The authorities try to break prisoners in order to make their incarceration easier. The ideal prisoner is quiet and passive and detaches himself from society. If you don't want to be broken, you must remain active—physically, psychologically, intellectually, and socially. You need to engage with your surroundings, inside prison and, as much as possible, outside of it. However, if you do this, you will inevitably come into conflict with the prison system. Being active in prison is synonymous with resisting in prison. It is the only way to retain your identity, dignity, and self-respect.

Extremely important during my imprisonment was the discovery of Michel Foucault's *Discipline and Punish*.[31] I was in isolation when I read the

---

31. Michel Foucault, *Discipline and Punish: The Birth of the Prison* (London: Allen Lane, 1977); French original: *Surveiller et punir. Naissance de la prison* (Paris: Gallimard, 1975).

book and it was a true revelation. It made me understand why prison is the way it is and why it functions the way it does. I also could relate Foucault's analysis of power and counterpower on the micro level directly to my prison experiences. The book helped me deal with the situation I was in. I turned from prisoner to researcher, doing a field study behind bars. In the end, the study had 2,400 pages and I was able to turn it both into a Master's thesis in Politics and a prisoners' survival manual.[32]

Since the authorities try to take control over your space and your time, you have to try to reclaim your space and your time. I managed to maintain relationships with my family, my friends, and the outside world, I did my studies, and when I was released I was in better physical shape than ever. I managed to turn the theft of space and time into something positive. That's why I don't look back at my time in prison with bitterness. It was not a traumatic experience, but an extreme one that allowed me a very close insight into the functioning of state power.

Many of my friends in Germany are surprised about the seemingly low sentences you got—not to even mention friends in the U.S.

Jan: Well, in this case, many Danes were surprised, too. There was a big public outcry over us not receiving higher sentences. Interestingly enough, the fact that we didn't commit the robberies for personal gain but for the support of Third World liberation movements was seen as an aggravating circumstance, not a mitigating one. We were even called "traitors to the nation." I find that rather curious.

Torkil: Prison sentences in Denmark are generally lower than in Germany or the U.S. I can't see someone in those countries who was involved in a robbery during which a policeman died receive the sentences we did. However,

---

32. Torkil Lauesen, *Fra forbedringshus til parkeringshus—magt og modmagt i Vridsløselille Statsfængsel* [From Rehabilitation Space to Storage Room: Power and Counterpower in the Vridsløselille State Prison] (Copenhagen: Hans Reitzel, 1998) and the prisoners' manual *Att leva i fängelse—en överlevnadshandbok för fångar* [Life in Prison: A Survival Manual for Prisoners] (Copenhagen: Andra chansen, 2000).

the police and the prosecution demanded higher sentences, they just didn't do a very good job. The original indictment contained twenty-two points, and in the end we were charged with less than a handful. It was probably good for us that we spent about a hundred days in the courtroom. They jurors saw and heard us day after day, and it became difficult for the police and the prosecution to maintain the image of us as "terrorists and cold-blooded murderers." In the end, the jurors decided to give us relatively mild sentences, which the police, the prosecution, and even the judges, were not happy with. It was particularly interesting to observe the police officers when the verdict was announced and one "not guilty" followed the other. They were very frustrated.

---

2 DET FRI AKTUELT · INDERSIDEN · TIRSDAG 20. SEPTEMBER 1994

BLEKINGEGADE-FOLK BAG FANGEAKTION

Tre af de dømte stor-røvere fra Blekingegade-sagen med i aktionsgruppe for Fangernes Dag

Af Klaus Dalgas og Jørgen Holst

Tre af de dømte stor-røvere fra den omtalte Blekingega-desagen har været med i et arrangement i den 14 mands store aktionsgruppe bag Fangernes Dag i går.

Det drejer sig om Niels Jørgensen, Thorkil Lauesen og Jan Weimann.

De tre røvere blev for to år siden dømt for det meget omtalte storrøveri på Købmagergade i København i 1988, hvor en ung politi-mand mistede livet. Senere blev der fundet et mindre arsenal af våben i gruppens

hovedkvarter i en lejlighed i Blekingegade i København.

De aktionerernes fangers talsmand, Preben Sørensen, erkender, at de tre stor-røvere har haft en væsentlig indflydelse på aktionsgrup-pens arbejde. Men han afviser, at de tre er hovedmæn-dene i den landsdækkende fangeaktion.

VELBEGAVEDE

»Jeg må indrømme, at de tre fra Blekingegade-sagen er særdeles velbegavede og velformulerede. De er absolut en gevinst for gruppen,« siger Preben Sørensen.

»Men alle 14 mand i talsgruppen har haft lige

meget at sige,« siger han.

Et af de tire hovedkrav i fangernes protest er netop, at give den femte mand i Blekingegadesagen, Marc Rudin, bedre fange-rettighe-der.

»Det er dog ikke til trevens skyld, at Marc Rudin er kommet med som et af vores hovedpunkter. Det ville vi have med under alle omstandighe-der,« siger Preben Sørensen fra Vridsløselille Statsfæng-sel.

blekingegade-folks skyld, at Marc Rudin er kommet med som et af vores hovedpunkter. Det ville vi have med under alle omstandighe-der,« siger Preben Sørensen fra Vridsløselille.

Schweizeren Marc Rudin sidder i øjeblikket i Horsens Statsfængsel, isoleret fra de andre fanger. Ifølge fange-bladet Brasen – der har Blekingegade manden Jan Weimann som redaktør – har man nægtet Marc Rudin

alle rettigheder med begrun-delsen, at han anses for potentiel flugt-truet, og at han er til fare for den danske stat.

EN NEDSLIDT MONDER

»Det er helt urimeligt. Vi synes, at Marc Rudin har fået en hård medfart og Det imrawat mange rettigheder. Og det vil vi have løst om,« siger talsmanden.

Preben Sørensen under-streger, at fangernes hoved-krav er få benådet livstidsfan-gen Palle Sørensen.

»Han er en nedslidt mand, der har siddet 29 år i fængsel, heraf 11 år i isolati-on. Derfor har vi også valgt Palle Sørensens årsdag som fangernes dag,« siger Pre-ben Sørensen.

FANGERNES FIRE HOVEDKRAV

1. **Benåd Palle Sørensen.**
Palle Sørensen er den person i det danske fæng-selssystem, der er blevet diskrimineret mest imod. Han er blevet et symbol på, hvor elendig vores retsstilling er i fængsler-ne.

2. **Nedlæg Afdeling B3 i**

Vridsløselille.
Det er lykkedes IG inf-nalforsorgen at isolere et mindre antal fanger (rock-ere red.) fra deres medfan-ger. Fangerne har gentag-ne gange påpeget, at der ikke er nogen reel grund til denne forkælsbehand-ling.

3. **Lad grønlændere af-**

sone i Grønland.
Det er på tide, at grøn-lændere får lov at afsone i deres eget miljø.

4. **Giv Marc Rudin nor-**
male fangerettigheder.
Marc Rudin er berøvet stort set alle normale ret-tigheder i Horsens Stats-fængsel, og denne forkæls-behandling må høre op.

DANMARKS FÆNGSLER

I Danmark er der 16 statsfængsler plus anstalten i Her-stedvester, som huser fanger i psykiatrisk behandling.

Desuden er der et antal arresthuse, hvor folk sid-der og venter på en fængselsdom.

Seks fængsler er luk-

kede fængsler, ti er åbne. I de lukkede og åbne fængsler er i dag indsat omkring 2680 fanger og i arresthusene omkring 1000.

Det samlede personale er 3500 personer.

Cellerne i fængsler og arresthuse udnyttes i øje-blikket op til 95 procent.

"Blekingegade Folks Behind Prisoners' Action." The box in the center reads: "The prisoners' four main demands: 1. Release Palle Sørensen. … 2. Close the Special Unit B3 in Vridsløselille State Prison. … 3. Let Greenlanders serve time in Greenland. … 4. Grant Marc Rudin his prisoners' rights."

Ekstra Bladet headline after the Blekingegade Group members acquitted of murder.
"Acquitted: The Police's Big Case against the Blekingegade Gang Blew Up like a Bag of Hot Air."

Jan: It was a tough battle, though, between the prosecution and the defense. Decisive for us was that we weren't convicted in the Rausing case because the jurors decided that we had voluntarily given up on the kidnapping plan— which was true. Had they found us guilty of this charge, we would have probably gotten eighteen years instead of ten.

Øvig Knudsen makes the abandonment of the kidnapping plan sound very dramatic: there was a meeting in the woods outside of Lund just hours before Rausing should be taken from his home. Is that an accurate description?

Jan: Let's just say that there was a late decision to call off the plan. The reasons were both of a personal and technical nature. It was all rather complex, but the bottom line was that we simply weren't able to do it.

Was it possible for you to coordinate your defense before the trial?

Jan: No, we were in isolation the whole time. But some of our lawyers were friends and in regular contact. We didn't all choose the same strategy. Torkil and Carsten decided to plead guilty to the Købmagergade robbery, while we others didn't plead anything. This ended up working well. I think it confused people, and the fact that two of us did give statements in court made us appear more human. It also made the case less dramatic. I think neither side had an interest in a politically charged trial. This was also different from the situation in Germany and the trials of the urban guerrilla members. In our case, the state wanted to keep the trial as "normal" as possible. It had no interest in creating martyrs. We were mistreated by a few individual cops, but, all in all, we were treated fairly. Our lawyers also did a very good job.

Torkil, why did you decide to plead guilty to the Købmagergade robbery?

Torkil: The evidence against me was overwhelming. Among the papers found at the Blekingegade apartment was a paper in my handwriting and with my fingerprints that outlined the dialogue I had with the guard at the post office yard just before the robbery. I would have been convicted either way. Pleading guilty simply allowed me to explain a few things, for example that the shot that was fired was not intended to harm anyone but to allow us to get away. I only described the sequence of events, not the roles that individuals played in them. This provided a counternarrative to the one presented by the police and the prosecution. The forensic evidence later confirmed my statement.

You have mentioned that you sat in isolation.

Torkil: That is true. For fifteen months. That was quite a long time.

What exactly does isolation mean in a Danish prison?

Torkil: You only have contact with your lawyer, the wardens, and perhaps the priest. You sit in a cell of twenty square feet for twenty-three hours a day. You have one hour in the yard, where you can move around in a small cage of sixty square feet. You can write and receive letters, but all of the communication is censored. You can listen to the radio and watch TV and loan books. I read a lot, mainly travel accounts and books on astrophysics—they helped me expand the small physical space I was in. You are allowed your own clothes, but not much else.

Jan: You have no one to talk to but yourself, the flies, and the spiders. In the beginning, we weren't allowed any visitors. Later, we got permission to receive a one-hour visit every other week. Eventually, we were allowed a one-hour visit each week. All visits were supervised; there were always two policemen present.

I also spend a year and a half in semi-isolation in different jails in and around Copenhagen. This was right after the sentencing, when the police requested to transfer me to Horsens State Prison, far away from my family. I filed a complaint. As a consequence, I found myself in jails where conditions were halfway between isolation and the normal Danish prison routine.

Was there public awareness about the isolation? In Germany, "isolation torture" was a big issue.

Jan: Yes, isolation in prisons was an issue in Denmark. But the debate didn't concern just us, Denmark got a lot of criticism for isolating prisoners in general. Amnesty International mentioned this several times in their reports.

Cell in Vridsløselille State Prison, 1992.

How did the authorities justify the measure?

Torkil: We were considered dangerous and did not cooperate with the police. The only statements any of us ever made were in court.

Jan: Well, and we were criminals. There wasn't much need to justify anything. Criminals get orders, not explanations. A few years after our release, however, new laws were implemented that make it harder to keep people in isolation for a long time.

How did the Danish left react to the trial and the sentences? Did you get much support?

Torkil: The majority of the Danish left distanced itself from us, while the Danish right tried to present us as a part of the left in order to discredit it. Some on the left also said that we had provided the intelligence service with an excuse for the repression of the left throughout the years. One has to remember that our case coincided with the fall of the "iron curtain" and the beginning of the "war on terror." For many, we symbolized the absolute

Vridsløselille State Prison photo sent by Torkil Lauesen to his wife Lisa, indicating his cell with the words "I live here."

worst: we were communists *and* terrorists. But we got support from parts of the radical left, people in the squatters' movement and the autonomous movement, and from friends and comrades. All in all, this amounted to a few hundred people. They demonstrated in front of the court building, sent letters, and supported us and our families financially. The support never ceased during our imprisonment. It is very important to know that you have support. Each letter makes you happy. I made many new friends while I was in prison.

You mentioned how the time in prison allowed you to observe state power from a unique perspective. How did you feel about the trial?

Torkil: There is a lot of ritual involved. It's all very theatrical: the judge sits on an elevated podium, the lawyers dress in special clothes, all that. There is also a special language being used. And not any language is accepted. The judge got very angry when we referred to our activities as "work." At one point, he yelled that he does not want to hear the term "work" one more time, since that was something that "honorable people" did in order to "make a living."

The whole security thing was a circus. We all sat in different jails, up to one hundred kilometers away from Copenhagen. Every single day we went to court, each one of us was picked up at six in the morning and rushed to the courthouse in supposedly inconspicuous passenger cars with several armed officers. Another car filled with armed officers was following us. The route changed every day. But this also had its entertaining moments. One time, the officers in my car got really nervous because another passenger car started following us—it turned out to be an unmarked police car that wanted to book us for speeding. Around the courthouse there were plenty of officers with Heckler & Koch machine guns.

All of this stood in strong contrast to the conduct of the state prosecutor Hans Christian Abildtrup, one of Denmark's most prominent, who smiled and nodded at us every morning. Once the trial was all over, he came up to me, patted me on the back, and said, "Thanks for the fight, Lauesen!"—as if the whole thing had been a sports competition. Some months later he was sentenced for DUI and lost his job.

The Parasite State Theory in Retrospect

Let us fast-forward to the present: the revolutionary promises of Third World liberation movements have largely vanished. Not many such movements are left, and only a fraction of them embrace socialism. World revolution hasn't come. What went wrong? Was capitalism too strong? Did you misjudge global economic developments? Did you have a wrong perception of the liberation movements?

Torkil: All of the above, I suppose. First, I think that Marxism in general has underestimated capitalism's ability to adapt and transform. Since the days of Marx, capitalism's "final crisis" has been announced many times. It was no different during the 1970s.

Second, I think the imperialist powers have learned a lot from the wars of the era. The U.S. has changed its tactics since Vietnam and has confronted liberation movements much more effectively since. The cases of Nicaragua and El Salvador are good examples, and so are the U.S. interventions in the Middle East.

Third, I think we overestimated the socialist element in the liberation movements, especially in its relation to the national element. Many of the movements were deeply nationalistic, but wore socialist colors. Not to be misunderstood: they weren't consciously deceiving, and the socialist attire wasn't fake; the socialist convictions just didn't run very deep. Socialism promised a better life and it gave people hope. But it wasn't at the core of the struggle, and national liberation rarely led to social liberation.

Fourth, I think we believed too strongly in the possibility of "delinking,"[33] that is, of a nation being able to detach itself from the global economic system and introducing a socialist economy within the framework of a liberated nation state. This is a much more daunting task than we thought. The pressure of the global market is enormous, and today, with neoliberalism and the ever-growing power of transnational companies, it is becoming even stronger.

Fifth, whatever one's opinion of the Soviet Union, its demise also meant

---

33. The term "delinking" was popularized among the anti-imperialist left by the Marxist economist Samir Amin and his book *Delinking: Toward a Polycentric World* (London: Zed, 1990); French original: *La déconnexion* (Paris: La Découverte, 1986).

the disappearance of the strategically most important counterpower to the U.S. No matter how you want to look at it, this was a strong blow to socialism.

Jan: Sadly, the model of the Soviet Union did not bring us closer to socialism. Successful liberation movements happily copied the political elements, like the one-party system, but very rarely was there a fundamental social transformation, a land reform, or expropriations.

Torkil: Many liberation movements with a socialist agenda gave up their principles once they seized power. The ANC in South Africa is perhaps the most prominent example. What is left of its socialist promises? Economically, South African society is more segregated today than it was under apartheid.

Jan: In fact, we never saw the ANC as particularly socialist. That was one of the reasons we didn't support it. The PAC had a very strong socialist rhetoric, but we didn't think it would ever have much influence. Therefore, we focused on a small group, the IRE, which we hoped would grow.

In a 2012 article about Samir Amin, Torkil wrote that anti-imperialism is nowadays considered "as 1970s as orange lamps and coffee tables in teak."[34] Is anti-imperialism really that outdated?

Torkil: Anti-imperialism itself is not outdated, it's just that the term has disappeared from political debate. At least in Denmark. There are remnants of anti-imperialist politics in organizations like the Internationalt Forum or Fighters and Lovers, but even there you hardly hear the term.[35]

---

34. Torkil Lauesen, "Tiden er ikke til sociale kompromisser" [It Is Not the Time for Social Compromises], *Gaia* no. 72, Spring 2012.

35. The Internationalt Forum is a network of Danish solidarity groups working against "oppression and exploitation worldwide" as well as "the capitalist world order" (http://www.internationaltforum.dk); it publishes the journal *Gaia—Tidskrift för international solidaritet* [Gaia: Journal for International Solidarity], to which Torkil Lauesen has contributed many articles. Fighters and Lovers is a Copenhagen-based group that has supported the PFLP and the FARC in Colombia by selling clothing, records, and perfume; in 2007, seven members of Fighters and Lovers were tried under the Danish anti-terrorism law and sentenced to suspended prison terms.

Why not? Obviously, the relations between the "metropole" and the "periphery"—or, in more contemporary terms, between the "Global North" and the "Global South"—are still characterized by enormous economic injustice.

Torkil: Of course the questions are still relevant, but the anti-imperialist movement, at least its socialist version, has practically disappeared as a political force. The empire still exists and unequal exchange still exists, but the social movement that organized against it under the banner of anti-imperialism does not. I suppose it has lost its historical moment. What's left is anti-imperialism under the banner of religion and reactionary politics.

Ahmadinejad is no anti-imperialist ally?

Torkil: For us, there has never been any valid anti-imperialism without a socialist base. We have always been primarily socialists. Anti-imperialism is important as a means to strengthen socialism, and if it doesn't serve that purpose, it is not relevant for us. The principle of "the enemy of my enemy is my friend" is way too simple—and dangerous.

Jan: This is not to say that we haven't made mistakes in our analysis. If we use the Iranian Revolution as an example, we were very supportive in the beginning. We believed that the socialist forces would come out strongest. Obviously, we were wrong, and if we had the chance to rewrite some of the articles we published in *Manifest*, we'd gladly take it. Of course, regimes like the one in Iran can weaken U.S. imperialism economically, but that in itself is not the point. As Torkil says, imperialism needs to be fought in order to make socialism possible. So if you don't do anything to introduce socialism—and, in fact, establish deeply reactionary regimes instead—then what kind of a contribution are you making? The religious regimes that claim anti-imperialist values have not liberated anyone. They are characterized by surveillance, repression, censorship, and so forth. None of the social problems have been solved.

I guess, today, discussions within the left that come closest to the old anti-imperialist topics are found in critiques of "neoliberalism" or "corporate globalization."

Torkil: That is true. Obviously, *Empire* by Hardt and Negri was a very widely read book.[36]

What did you think of it?

Torkil: I thought it was inspiring. The description of the decreasing significance of the nation state and the arrival of an "empire" consisting of transnational corporations, transnational institutions like the World Trade Organization, and the leading imperialist countries' political and military apparatuses is convincing. I do not deplore the nation state losing significance. Nationalism has always been a problem for socialism and anti-imperialism. You can also see this in the terminology. In the eighteenth and nineteenth centuries, imperialism played an important role in the creation of the "nation" and a "national people." Colonial racism set the "civilized" peoples of Europe against the "uncivilized," "savage" peoples of Africa, Latin America, and Asia. The terms "nation," "people," and "race" are all closely connected. Then, during the second half of the nineteenth century, nationalist sentiments grew rapidly within the European workers' movement. Communism's original internationalism was weakened. Imperialism had an enormous success in dividing the world's proletariat into different, competing factions. Many workers in the imperialist countries identified so strongly with their nation that they were ready to fight in imperialist—and "inter-imperialist"—wars. Think of Rosa Luxemburg's passionate but ineffective appeals to internationalism during World War I.

In anti-colonial and anti-imperialist struggles, however, nationalism has also played a progressive role as a bulwark against the most powerful nations' global domination. In the form of national liberation movements, nationalism was able to defeat colonial and imperialist rule. But once nationalist sentiments were no longer used to protect communities against enemies from the outside, in other words, once they turned inwards, the notions of national identity, security, and unity became tools of oppression. Protection and oppression are often hard to distinguish. It seems that many successful national liberation movements got stuck in this dilemma: they found

---

36. Michael Hardt and Antonio Negri, *Empire* (Cambridge, MA: Harvard University Press, 2000).

themselves either embracing an oppressive and isolated nationalism or adapting to the global neoliberal market, as in the South African case.

By addressing these questions, *Empire* opens up perspectives for renewed global resistance—in a way, the book takes us back to the internationalism of Marx and Lenin. At the same time, I don't think that Hardt and Negri offer any concrete answers to the question of what to do. They have no suggestions for concrete steps in the here and now, and no long-term strategies either. At this point, they prefer to take on the role of academics, leaving it to the "activists" to figure these things out. But a political theory that offers no concrete suggestions for political practice is a weak theory. There are still too many philosophers interpreting the world, while the real challenge remains to change it.

What's left of the parasite state theory?

Torkil: A lot. We are not talking about an obscure idea from the 1970s. The core of the parasite state theory remains highly relevant. Even recent academic work proves this, for example John Smith's *Imperialism and the Globalisation of Production*, Timothy Kerswell's *The Global Division of Labour and the Division in Global Labour*, and Zak Cope's *Divided World Divided Class*—all studies that have been published within the last few years.[37]

I think there is still strong empirical evidence for the connection between imperialism and the labor aristocracy. Plenty of data confirms the increasing gap between the living standards in our part of the world and the ones in the Third World. About half of the world's population lives on less than two U.S. dollars a day. The average wage difference between the OECD countries[38] and the rest of the world is about 11 to 1. Today, 80 percent of the world's industrial workers are located in the Third World, generating superprofits for transnational corporations and cheap goods for the labor aristocracy in

---

37. John Smith, *Imperialism and the Globalisation of Production* (PhD thesis, University of Sheffield, 2010); Timothy Kerswell, *The Global Division of Labour and the Division in Global Labour* (PhD thesis, Queensland University of Technology, 2011); Zak Cope, *Divided World Divided Class* (Montreal: Kersplebedeb, 2012).

38. See p. 61 n. 41.

the imperialist countries. Zak Cope has calculated that in 2009, the value transferred to the OECD countries from the rest of the world amounted to 6,500 billion U.S. dollars. As citizens of one of the world's richest countries, we have been privileged enough to travel and see the results of such inequality with our own eyes.

In the 1970s, the Third World mainly had significance as an exporter of raw materials: metals, minerals, and agricultural products such as coffee, tea, fruits, etc. Industrial production was weak and limited to low-technology products such as clothes and shoes. But over the last twenty-five years, this has changed. The Third World has experienced a massive industrialization, with production reaching from heavy industry to advanced electronics. Productivity is at least as high as in the old industrial metropole. This, inevitably, changes the global balance of power. Today, the Third World plays a much more important economic and political role than it did in the 1970s. Africa is lagging behind, but if you look at China or India, their voices become more important with each big international meeting.

This is a process that we did not foresee in the 1970s; the logistical obstacles seemed too big: communication, transport, cultural differences, etc. We also thought that the working classes of the metropole would fight hard to prevent the relocation of production. We were wrong, and now we are facing very different economic conditions. This also has a huge impact on the possibilities of revolutionary politics. The colonialism of old is gone. Modern imperialism is not international but transnational.

Jan: I agree that many things have changed, but the basic global structure remains the same. It is evident that the hopes we had for a global revolutionary transformation sparked by Third World liberation movements remained unfulfilled, but global economic inequality is still the most striking of capitalism's contradictions. Production might have moved to the Third World, but profits are still moving to the metropole.

Torkil: If we take the purchasing power of Copenhagen with its one million inhabitants, then it equals the purchasing power of Tanzania with forty-six million people. Neoliberalism allows you to move production to where wages are low and then ship the products to where purchasing power is high. That way you profit on both ends. You can send a design for a Nike sneaker as a PDF to Vietnam, where you get the sneakers produced for next to nothing before moving them in modern containers to the U.S., where you can sell them for a multiple of the production costs. Making profit has never been easier. Once you have functioning logistics, modern technology, and safe transport, you are set. In the metropole, production is no longer key—what counts is design and marketing. The technologies are very different to the 1970s, but they perpetuate, and even strengthen, the same patterns of exploitation. At the time, we spoke of "parasite states." Today, we might want to speak of "producer states" and "consumer states."

Revolutionary Perspectives Then and Now

During the 1970s, you criticized most leftist organizations very harshly. Do you still have the same criticism?

Torkil: In terms of focusing on the relative privileges of the working class in Western Europe, I don't think much has changed. The agenda of the main left-wing parties and trade unions remains the same. Today, they are focused on the defense of the welfare state within a national and capitalist framework. This is not a struggle that aids or supplements the struggle in the Third World. It is not a struggle for socialism. Even the old communist parties have lost any internationalist perspective. If workers vote for them it is not because they want socialism, but because they believe that these parties are better able to secure their wages than the Social Democrats. The whole political spectrum has moved to the right, and the interests of the Western working class are still tied to the interests of capital.

In today's Europe, we are witnessing three major strategies to gain the political support of the working class:

1. Neoliberal Social Democracy: The old workers' parties have become almost indistinguishable from other neoliberal parties. They stress the need to train a national labor force in order to occupy key functions within the new international division of labor. This shall guarantee the protection of the labor force's privileges. The Social Democrats and other social-liberal parties also try to create the best

possible framework for this: the right infrastructure, taxation, etc. There is no class perspective left, and the focus lies exclusively on national interests. All nations are doing the same, which leads to a neoliberal rat race, in which national working classes are trying to avoid ending up at the bottom.

2. Right-wing nationalism: Forces on the right end of the political spectrum use nationalism as a tool to fight globalization, which they portray as the main threat to the Western working class's privileges. The right promises to defend jobs by implementing strict immigration laws and militarizing national borders. Today, right-wing nationalist parties are often the biggest workers' parties. The left explains this as a result of "false consciousness" and "political naiveté." Nothing could be further from the truth. The right-wing parties profit from very conscious class politics. Their success has to be understood in the context of the global class structure created by imperialism.

3. The defense of the social welfare state: This is the strategy that the old communist parties have inherited from the Social Democrats. It indicates a clear goodbye to any radical approach and the final compromise with reformist parliamentarianism. To speak of revolution or the abolition of private property always leads left-wing parliamentarians to argue that this will "scare away the voters." In the 1970s, some of these parties might have still seen themselves as the parliamentarian voice of the extraparliamentary left. Today, all they are interested in are sociological studies helping them to optimize their votes and to win over disgruntled Social Democrats.

It is easy to point out that the right-wing arguments are false. They claim that we have to protect our riches because we have created them with our own sweat and tears, while poverty in the Third World is the result of cultural backwardness and laziness. Of course the opposite is true: it is the Third World that has created our riches. It was Europeans who plundered South America, who transported millions of slaves to North America, and who colonized Africa and Asia.

However, the approach of the left-wing parties is also wrong, or, in any case, short-sighted. If the Western working classes do not want to compete with the workers of China or Brazil (a competition they might very well lose), then they must develop a global perspective and fight the racial and cultural hierarchy of nations as well as the enormous gaps in living standards. The way forward, the way towards socialism, lies in a struggle against global inequality, not in narrow nationalism. Let me quote something from an address prepared by Marx for the 1867 congress of the First International. Speaking about the situation in England, he stated: "In order to oppose their workers, the employers either bring in workers from abroad or else transfer manufacture to countries where there is a cheap labor force. Given this state of affairs, if the working class wishes to continue its struggle with some chance of success, the national organizations must become international."[39] Marx knew how important wage differences were—and, at the time, they were significantly smaller than they are today.

Marx's quote still holds true. What socialist politics demand today is an uncompromising global perspective. I understand that this might not bring many votes. That, however, can't be the measure of socialist politics. Sometimes, I miss the radicalism and the global perspective that were part of the left in the 1970s. Not because of nostalgia, but because these aspects seem more necessary than ever if we want another world.

As you've stated, the revolutionary hopes of the 1970s remained largely unfulfilled. Where does revolutionary hope come from today?

Torkil: One has to understand what a revolutionary situation is. This has always been the key question. The collaboration between KAK and China ended in 1969, because China saw a revolutionary situation in Western Europe and we didn't.

For a revolutionary situation, it is not enough that the masses want a different society. The ruling class must also be unable to maintain and defend the status quo. The masses must *no longer want* to follow the same path, and the ruling class must *no longer be able* to.

---

39. Torkil Lauesen refers to an address prepared for the Congress of the International Workingmen's Association in Lausanne 1867. The address was written by a committee appointed by the General Council. Karl Marx was one of four committee members. For the entire text and background information, see http://www.marxists.org.

Jan: During the October Revolution, the masses didn't want "socialism," they wanted bread. They were in the middle of an imperialist war and famine. They were destitute. The revolution became a question of survival. It succeeded because the old regime could no longer defend itself.

In Germany, the situation was similar, but the ruling class managed to hand power to the Social Democrats, who crushed the radical currents under the banner of socialist development. That was a brilliant move on the part of the ruling class and it prevented a true revolution.[40]

Torkil: Others on the left have accused us of propagating the "immiseration thesis." However, this needs a bit of historical context.

The term "immiseration thesis" was introduced by Eduard Bernstein, the father of reformist socialism, in the late nineteenth century. Bernstein rejected Marx's claim that capitalism led to increasing wealth for the few and increasing poverty for the many. According to Bernstein, the struggles for higher wages and social reforms had increased the living standard of the German working class significantly, which proved that Marx was wrong and that reformism was the way forward. However, Bernstein acknowledged neither the growing gap between the bourgeoisie and the working class nor the pauperization of those on the periphery of capitalist development, mainly the people in the colonies, but also in Russia. By focusing exclusively on the relative increase of living standards among German workers, Bernstein failed to see the essential truth in Marx's analysis.

When we insisted that Marx was right, we didn't simply mean that "things have to get worse in order to get better." This is nothing that Marx or Engels ever meant. The point is therefore not to argue that things have to get worse. The point is to define moments of possibility for radical change. In an 1885 article about the situation in England, Engels wrote that socialism will return when the country's industrial monopoly ends and the English working class finds itself on equal terms with the working classes of other nations.[41] We are

40. For a history of the German Revolution from a radical perspective, see Gabriel Kuhn (ed.), *All Power to the Councils! A Documentary History of the German Revolution of 1918–1919* (Oakland: PM Press, 2012).

41. Friedrich Engels, "England 1845 und 1885" [England 1845 and 1885], *Die neue Zeit* no. 6, June 1885.

talking about classical Marxist questions: What are the objective conditions for social change? Who has an objective interest in social change? What is the state of capitalism? Will capitalism be able to solve its crisis, or will the crisis escalate?

Jan: The basis of your theory has to be material reality. This hasn't changed. If your theory is not based on material reality, you become a dreamer, and fantasy replaces theory. As a dreamer, you can proclaim whatever you want. But transforming society has nothing to do with wishful thinking. Useful theory must be based on the analysis of the actual material conditions.

Torkil: I believe that the key aspect in the current situation is the industrialization of the Third World and the emergence of a new working class, a new industrial proletariat. Just as the European working class did in the nineteenth century, the new working classes of China, India, Vietnam, Brazil, and Mexico will demand social justice. There will be new social conflicts, and they will be framed in economic terms, not in the cultural and national terms of the 1970s. The first round of anti-imperialist struggles was mainly nationalist. The next round will be mainly anti-capitalist.

Why are you so certain that the struggles will no longer be framed in nationalist terms? Because the role of the nation state has been weakened? That doesn't necessarily weaken nationalistic sentiments, does it? Sometimes, the opposite seems true.

Jan: It's a complex issue. The nation state will continue to be evoked as a bulwark of defense against "foreign influence" of all sorts. But I think there are two strong indications that the national aspect will be weaker in upcoming struggles. One is indeed the shift in global politics and the global economy. The role of the nation state has, in fact, been weakened. This also means that the front lines of social struggles have shifted. The other indication is that many new independent countries have emerged over the last decades. These include former colonies in the Third World as well as former Soviet and Yugoslav republics, and others. The process has made the "national question" less urgent overall—even if some struggles, for example the Palestinian one, are still very much framed in such terms.

Torkil: As I've said before, I don't think there is any reason to bemoan the fact that the nation state has lost significance. This development opens up new possibilities. But in order to seize them, we must really think beyond the national framework and develop a global consciousness. I believe we are heading the right way. In the 1970s, the oil crisis already made it very clear how dependent we have become on one another, and in recent decades, the environmental movement has contributed in many ways to widening this understanding. Meanwhile, activists have been organizing World Social Forums, and migration has become one of the most important political issues globally. The changes are also expressed on the legal level. Take the International Court of Justice in The Hague, for example. Nation states refusing to subject themselves to such institutions meet with increasingly strong criticism. Even the USA is not exempt—the Guantánamo prison camp, for example, is condemned almost universally. This is encouraging, even if the true "pariah states" are still those in opposition to Western interests.

The consequence of these developments is not necessarily stronger global solidarity, but the developments are a precondition for stronger global solidarity—as well as for more democracy in global affairs.

Yes, there will be nationalistic backlashes. For many, nationalism remains an easy answer to complex problems. It is therefore crucial for the left not to fall into the trap of using nationalist sentiments to oppose global capital and its institutions. Otherwise, our resistance won't differ much from that of the right.

When defining a revolutionary situation, a capitalist crisis still seems very central to you. But isn't capitalism going through a crisis right now?

Torkil: The recent crisis was a financial one, mainly concerning the real estate market. In Europe, only Greece and perhaps Spain have been significantly affected.

Jan: When we say "crisis" we mean a development that significantly affects the living conditions of the workers. What we have seen in recent years is more of a "recession." Even a crisis like the one in the 1930s did not lead to major uprisings, although the unemployment rate was very high and people relied on handouts, free meals, etc.

So where can a "real" global crisis of capitalism come from today? From a crisis in Third World countries instigated by new revolutionary working class movements?

Jan: Well, if there is a crisis in Vietnam, and you can go produce the same thing under the same conditions in Malaysia, then capitalism won't be affected. But if we look at significant global powers, such as China, then a crisis there will inevitably affect us all. Once our profits and living standards are affected, that is, once we can no longer buy goods as cheaply as we have become used to, we will no longer be able to ignore this and things will start moving. Plus, there are other factors to consider: global warming, overpopulation, migration, etc. It is even possible that production in the Third World will collapse. That would be a huge problem for capitalism. Look at what seemingly small things can do: a simple real estate crisis can cause serious unemployment.

But crises do not necessarily lead to progressive change. Often, reactionary forces benefit. How can that be avoided?

Torkil: Socialism has to be seen as an attractive and realistic solution to people's problems. Considering the historical track record of real socialism, that is not a given. To say that some mistakes have been made and that we should just try the same experiment again, won't help. I don't think that's possible, and I believe very few people do. It is mandatory to formulate new and concrete ideas of what a socialist economy should look like. These ideas have to be based on people's experiences. Again, the organization of democratic socialism must appear both attractive and realistic.

Things aren't entirely hopeless. At least people are talking about socialism again, even if it is often in the form of a "lifeboat socialism," that is, a safety buoy in times of ecological and economic disasters.

Do you see anyone contributing to a new socialist vision?

Torkil: I think the Zapatistas provide an example. They are expressing socialist ideas in a new language. They are also anti-imperialists, although this might be anti-imperialism 2.0. In any case, the perspective of their struggle is global, not national.

We can see similar tendencies in many struggles, addressing everything from privatization to copyright issues to the "discursive struggles" that Foucault has written about. Of course there are important struggles happening on the governmental and institutional level, but there are many small struggles in everyday life that concern very basic questions about what is good and bad, right and wrong, and so forth. All of them include the potential to strengthen socialist ideals. Here, too, the Zapatistas are a good example. They have a Foucauldian understanding of power: the micro level is very important; they don't see power concentrated in institutions.

The socialist movements that have recently experienced success in the Third World seem to be mainly peasant-based Maoist movements, for example in Nepal and in parts of India. How does this fit in with your focus on the new Third World proletariat?

Torkil: It is natural that regions with a strong peasant base have strong peasant movements. Peasants are arguably the most exploited sector in the Third World today, and land reform is still a major issue. However, I am not sure how much of a model they can be. It is also clear that their Maoism has very little to do with today's China. It seems more like a Maoism of the 1970s.

Jan: Of course peasants will remain an important factor, but the new proletariat is expanding fast and includes a strong rural proletariat. In China, you have poor migrant workers who travel thousands of kilometers to find work.

Let us take a concrete example of recent unrest in the midst of an economic crisis, the so-called Arab Spring. The way things are looking now, this has not strengthened progressive forces.

Torkil: One thing that the Arab Spring has demonstrated is the importance of organized political movements. The Islamists have come out strong because they were well organized. They currently have the organizational skills that the socialists had in the 1970s, and also the same strong ideological foundation. Websites, SMS chains, and tent cities are not enough for radical social change. Some of the experiences from the disciplined and vanguardist organizations from the 1970s might still be useful here, even if they must not be copied uncritically, of course.

Jan: I think you have to look at the specific circumstances of the Arab Spring. While economic conditions might have triggered the uprisings, the main agenda was democratization. People rallied against authoritarian rule and seemed convinced that democracy, in the sense of the Western parliamentarian model, would make things better. That the protests were fueled by new communication technologies fits the picture: the Internet and mobile phones have an aura of democracy that spills over into politics. So far, so good. But no one formulated any social programs. And the belief that life will be the same as in France or Germany once you get rid of an authoritarian ruler is an illusion. If we take Egypt as an example, hardly anyone demanded more than Mubarak's resignation. There were no demands for a land reform or other substantial political and economic changes. Under such circumstances, it is not surprising if you end up with new people driving the old apparatus. People do not rise up because they want democracy or any other abstraction. They rise up because they want a better life. Democracy only becomes an abstract image they can project their hopes into, but that's not the same as having your hopes fulfilled.

Why would it be different in China?

Torkil: China has a tradition of working-class organizing, a communist party, and radical collective action. I think that people in China know that you can't change the system with a Facebook account and a sleeping bag on Tiananmen Square. There is a deeper understanding of social change.

Jan: I cannot promise that it will be different, but there is a strong sense of pragmatism in China. This is also true for the Communist Party. If there is a problem, no one consults the Marxist dictionary. People develop practical solutions instead. China's current economic system is a case in point. It's not the kind of free market system that we have in Europe. It's a system that integrates a free market into a tightly controlled state apparatus. It's very unique. This also means that the tensions that will arise between those defending the status quo and those demanding social change will have far-reaching effects.

You talk about far-reaching effects, globalization, and the importance of political organizing. What does this mean for global forms of resistance? Aren't they necessary in light of the current political and economic developments?

Jan: We need new forms of revolutionary organizing, that is true. Back in the day, we believed in the revolution spreading from the Third World to the metropole with the Russian Revolution as a shining example. We had a very simple and linear idea of socialist development. Today, we realize that things are more complicated than that. Our views are far less deterministic. I think that many different forms of solidarity can arise globally—around labor issues, but also around climate issues and others. We are already witnessing developments that no one would have thought possible ten years ago. Numerous Latin American governments espouse a language that is reminiscent of the anti-imperialism of the 1970s. They criticize unequal exchange. And we are talking about governments that were voted in by parliamentary elections. And they cooperate, for example in ALBA.[42]

Migration is another important issue. In Denmark and in other European countries, most migrants are quickly integrated into the labor market, but in the U.S., for example, you have millions of illegal immigrants who work for very low wages and whose living standards can't be compared to those of the old U.S. working class. This creates tensions that will inevitably lead to widespread social conflict.

Torkil: Neoliberalism leads to strong economic polarization everywhere, both in the metropole and in the Third World. As much as you have a new middle class, and even billionaires, in China and India, you have new poverty in North America and Western Europe, particularly affecting illegal immigrants and undocumented workers.

Jan: In addition, the old struggles haven't disappeared. Of course it's easy to point out the failures of the liberation movements. The PFLP does not hold power in Palestine. But if you always look at things from the most negative angle, you might as well stop doing anything. Even if Mugabe has "betrayed" the revolution in Zimbabwe, it was still a step forward when the country got rid of the white colonialists' regime. The same is true for FRELIMO taking

---

42. The Alianza Bolivariana para los Pueblos de Nuestra América (ALBA) was founded upon the initiative of the late Venezuelan president Hugo Chávez in 2004. In 2013, ALBA consisted of the following member states: Antigua and Barbuda, Bolivia, Cuba, Dominica, Ecuador, Nicaragua, Saint Vincent and the Grenadines, Saint Lucia, and Venezuela.

power in Mozambique and for many similar cases. The struggle in Palestine continues as well, even if socialist ideas have taken a backseat.

I guess my question is: how can the many sites of resistance be connected in order to respond to the global force of capital? Can unions play a role here, especially when one puts a focus on workers in the Third World?

Jan: I am skeptical with respect to the global union movement. The interests of the national unions are too different. A union's primary duty is to defend the interests of its members. But the interests of the Danish working class are still very different from the interests of the Ethiopian working class. In the metropole, unions mainly fight to defend privileges, they don't fight for global social justice. A Danish union can't demand lower wages for its members and higher wages for African workers. It just doesn't work that way.

Torkil: In general, I do believe that union politics will be important, because they will play a role in the process of Third World workers organizing. But the international union movement is still largely dominated by unions from the imperialist countries, so I don't think there is much potential there—even if there have been some progressive trends since the International Trade Union Confederation has tried to leave the shadows of the Cold War behind.[43] Of course, Third World unions are making themselves heard more and more, but I think it will still be a long time before they have a strong global impact. Unequal exchange is still not a central issue for international trade unionism. People are rightfully outraged over differences between men's and women's pay, but at the same time no one seems to bother about the enormous differences between First World and Third World wages. If unions can't move beyond a nationalist perspective, it will be very hard for them to play a decisive role in the global struggle for socialism.

---

43. The International Trade Union Confederation (ITUC), the world's largest trade union federation, was founded in 2006 as a merger of the International Confederation of Free Trade Unions (ICFTU) and the World Confederation of Labour (WCL). According to its website (http://www.ituc-csi.org), the ITUC "represents 175 million workers in 156 countries and territories and has 315 national affiliates" in April 2013.

In the book Unequal Exchange and the Prospects of Socialism, *which was first published by M-KA in Danish in 1983, you had a chapter entitled "What Can Communists in the Imperialist Countries Do?"[44] It was five pages long. How would you respond to that question today?*

Torkil: Well, there you can see the Leninist influence. Whenever there was a problem, Lenin made an analysis and presented five "What to Do" pages. Mao Zedong did the same. They were fairly successful. Others who tried this, like Jose Maria Sison in the Philippines, were not.[45] Perhaps we weren't so good at it either.

Does this mean that you won't answer the question?

Jan: You are talking to two individuals and not to a political organization. We have no organizational unity or strategy, only personal opinions. Torkil might have read many books, but we still don't have any answers. I agree that global connections are necessary, but I would also say that every time someone acts in the spirit of solidarity a step in the right direction is made. There are many initiatives that are not necessarily revolutionary, but still contribute to social conditions that make positive development easier. The more actions we see headed in that direction, the better things will become in the long run, even if the establishment of socialism seems far away and will require bigger efforts than single-issue campaigns.

I still like the slogan, "Solidarity is something you can hold in your hands." This can always be a guiding principle for political action, even when you lack answers to the big questions. Solidarity is always needed, and there are always possibilities to express it in concrete ways. However, analysis, theory, and propaganda are also needed to encourage solidarity, so this aspect of political activism doesn't lose its importance.

---

44. The chapter is included in this volume in the "Documents" section.

45. Jose Maria Sison founded the Communist Party of the Philippines and its armed wing, the New People's Army, in 1968–1969. Since 1987 he has been living in exile in the Netherlands.

Do you have any concrete examples for how to express solidarity today? Or for which movements to support?

Torkil: In China, I think it's important to support left-wing currents within the Communist Party, independent working-class movements, and all initiatives that fight for a global instead of a national perspective in union politics. In the Middle East and in North Africa it is crucial to support the progressive forces that remain. I hope that the Islamist wave will subside, but liberal democracy will not help the poor farmers and the unemployed in the region either. If the left manages to reorganize itself and to formulate ideas for fundamental changes in property relations, I think that socialist politics can be revived. The situation is very fragile and seemingly small things can have a great effect. Finally, I think we must support what is left of the movements from the 1970s in Palestine, in the Western Sahara, in Colombia, and certainly in Mexico. Some other questions need more investigation: Is it, for example, possible to connect the struggle in Greece with anti-imperialist politics and a broad global perspective? In any case, none of these struggles can be fought successfully without an understanding of global capitalism's class structures and a commitment to a global equality in living standards.

Jan: I think it is also important to experiment with new forms of collaboration; collaboration between groups that aren't used to working together: environmental organizations with trade unions, consumer cooperatives with producer alliances, etc. In Europe, I think the struggle against racism has a high priority. Different ethnic groups are turned into scapegoats for the current social problems. Whenever a population is divided, right-wing forces benefit and the situation will become even more difficult for progressive and socialist movements.

Maybe we are in a phase that needs another Cultural Revolution. Mao wanted all ideas to be expressed in order to filter out the best for the future. A day will come—and perhaps many days—when socialism will be a relevant political force again, able to limit capitalism's power. It would be nice if one could point out a single way to get us there—but that's an impossible thing to do.

You have repeatedly stressed that you see things in a more complex manner today than forty years ago. Yet, sometimes, it seems hard not to envy people who have clear political ideas, visions, and strategies. It seems very rare today. Isn't that also a problem?

Torkil: I'm not going to lie: it was great to have an all-encompassing theory and practice that you believed in. You had a complete worldview, which was wonderful. However, that was modernity. Today, we live in postmodern times...

Seriously speaking, I don't think there is any way for us to return to a world that existed forty years ago. I understand the envy, but believe me, if you got the chance, you wouldn't feel comfortable with the clear-cut answers we felt we had. I think hardly anyone would these days. We have entered new times, and new times require new forms of politics.

The following quote is from David Gilbert's book Love and Struggle, *which came out in 2012— "It seems to me that the central problem/tension is still between imperialism and the conditions of life throughout the Third World, even if it won't necessarily be fought or in the form of national liberation struggles"*[46]*—do you agree?*

Torkil: Yes, that's a nice quote. I would agree. Despite the anti-imperialist liberation struggles disappearing during the 1980s, the main contradiction in the world remains the one between the rich capitalist countries in the North and the exploited countries in Asia, Africa, and Latin America. Future anti-imperialist struggles are inevitable.

---

46. David Gilbert was a longtime member of the Weather Underground. He is serving a sentence of seventy-five years to life in New York for his involvement in the so-called Brink's Robbery of 1981, a joint action of the Black Liberation Army and former Weather Underground members. His autobiographical account *Love and Struggle: My Life in SDS, the Weather Underground, and Beyond* was published in 2012 by PM Press.

DOCUMENTS

Socialism and the Bourgeois Way of Life

Gotfred Appel

This article originally appeared as "Socialisme og borgerlig levevis" in Kommunistisk Orientering *no. 7, March 21, 1968. It was published in English, together with other articles from* Kommunistisk Orientering, *in the pamphlet* There Will Come a Day... Imperialism and the Working Class *(Copenhagen: Futura, 1971).*

It is immediately evident that the principal class contradiction in the parasite state of Denmark has always been and still is the contradiction between the bourgeoisie and the proletariat—between the class which is in power, and which has ownership of the means of production on the one hand, and on the other hand that class which is the child of the capitalist big industry, and which has nothing but its labour power to sell.

But that does *not* necessarily mean that *always and under all circumstances* the bourgeoisie is grossly oppressing and exploiting the proletariat. The technical development as a whole, the gigantic, modern production machine in the developed capitalist world as a whole are built on exploitation, on the value-creating labour of the workers, yes—but in the imperialist countries the whole of this development has mainly taken place on the basis of a vigorous exploitation, *not* of the workers of the imperialist countries themselves, but of the working people of the colonial and dependent countries.

Today the factor of exploitation is present in Danish capitalist society, but it does not take up the dominant position. Today the factor of bribery is dominating the relation between the bourgeoisie and the proletariat. This factor of bribery has had its imprint on the attitude of the working class *as a whole.*

As a result of the factor of bribery, as a result of the enormous growth of capitalist industry, as a result of social-democratic reformism and modern revisionism the working class' habits of life, its demands in life, its dreams and expectations—and even the means used by it to attain them—are bourgeois, bourgeois to the marrow!

You cannot just say that as far as material standard of living is concerned we have "gone too far ahead" compared to the people out there. You cannot say that we have to "wait for them a little", until we can proceed together with them.

In the parasite consumer's society of Denmark we have not gone too far "ahead". We have gone in the wrong direction. We have gone in a bourgeois direction, in a direction which is one hundred per cent bourgeois individualistic.

Progress—material as well as cultural—will take quite another direction under socialism. No one can say exactly what road it will take—the working class will have to and is going to pave it itself—but it is *not* going to be the bourgeois road, it is *not* going to be the road, which we have followed for the past many decades.

Of course, Lenin was right when he once said that it was easier to carry out the socialist revolution in Russia than it was going to be in Western Europe, but that in return it would be easier in Western Europe than in the Soviet Union to build the material industrial basis of socialism. Of course we shall never start our socialist construction on the same level—technically, materially—as for instance India.

But nevertheless when that time comes we shall find ourselves in a situation, where we shall have to build our socialist Denmark with *diligence and thrift*. The glare of advertising and the whole of the gigantic industry behind the noise, will stop. The hurlyburly of fashion will come to an end, the status symbols will lose their importance and their value—and no longer will there be such a difference in the standard of living from country to country that it will be cheaper for Danes to go by jet-plane to Mallorca than have one's holiday on the [Danish island of] Bornholm!

When we *know* that a fundamental change will take place in the way of life of the working class first of all and then of the working people, a fundamental change in the demands they make of life and their personal needs, when we *know* that we have not gone too far "ahead" in the direction the whole of mankind will take, but that we have gone in the wrong direction—when we *know* that, should we not tell the working class? Should we not, as part of the revolutionary agitation and propaganda, tell the working class, that with absolute certainty the day is bound to come when the class must not only acquire the ideology—Marxism—which is its own, in the true sense of the word, but that it must also create its own attitude towards life and educate the whole of the working population in this world outlook and this ideology, and this attitude?

Or should we, as the revisionists want us to do, carry on the efforts to lead the working class in the direction, which we *know* to be wrong? Should we assist and lead it in the efforts to get still more of the "benefits", which the bourgeoisie has succeeded in making the working class consider "benefits"? Should we lead it to satisfy still more of the "needs" which the bourgeoisie has imposed on it through the glare of advertisement of the consumer's society? Should we be really "revolutionary", even, and help the working class invent *new* needs of exactly the same kind?

Thus the question is posed:

Should we strive to lead the workers in the struggle for higher wages, shorter working hours, mobilize it to demand more bourgeois "social benefits", more "spare time benefits", to satisfy its bourgeois needs for "leisure"?

Or should we openly call it swindle and deception to promise the workers things which we know they cannot get? Should we openly call it pandering to the bourgeois way of thinking, to the bourgeois strivings in the working class, and straight out declare that it must be fought against, and that this fight is one of the preconditions of the socialist revolution?

Should we not openly say that the whole of this struggle for the fulfillment of bourgeois needs is leading the working class directly away from a socialist way of thinking? That the trade union activity at the *present* level of development of the parasite state is *directly* harmful and a hindrance to the struggle for socialism?

In the present situation, where the factor of bribery is dominating in relation to the factor of exploitation, and where the working class as a whole—organizationally, politically and ideologically—has made itself the ally of the bourgeoisie in order *together with* the bourgeoisie to preserve capitalist society—in this situation it is the main task of the revolutionary communists to break down this bourgeois way of thinking in the working class. The task is to point out precisely that the way of thinking which is characteristic of the class as a whole, *is* bourgeois.

We have to start an ideological offensive against the bourgeois, reformist and revisionist ideology and all its manifestations and effects. We must take the offensive in order, through this destruction, to spread an understanding of the factor of bribery and the objectively existing road of development, which *no one* and *nothing* can halt. We have to build up revolutionary strength for the day of battle to come.

Of course, the very nature of the situation dictates that these ideas will not take root among the great masses of workers and working people right away. But gradually the factor of bribery *will* diminish. Gradually we *shall* come into a situation where first of all the working class will be an exploited class—if it does not happen more suddenly in connection with a holocaust of crises and wars!

In the course of this development more and more people will have their eyes opened—if revolutionary communists prove able to conduct their ideological, political and organizational struggle correctly, and if they are able constantly to sum up experience, correct mistakes made, and deepen their understanding together with the changes in this reality and through this to create close links with these increasing numbers of people.

Above all, it will be an ideological struggle in the working class itself. It will be a struggle against all bourgeois tendencies which will hamper the workers' understanding of the fact that the coming national crisis is in their own long-term and deepest interest, and which will also tend to draw the workers away from solidarity with the fighting peoples of Asia, Africa and Latin America and over to the side of its "own" capitalists.

It is going to be a hard and difficult struggle. But as the inevitable economic development proceeds, and as the "cosy" life of the labour aristocracy, which has been built on the backs of millions and millions of human beings, disappears, this development will mobilize more and more people. At a certain point, the struggle will also become an economic struggle to defend the very means of existence, and in the end it will also be a political revolutionary struggle for power in society.

One day the situation will exist when the dominant position of bourgeois ideology and bourgeois way of life among the working class will be broken down to a sufficient degree and replaced with Marxism applied to Danish reality, and where the contradiction between the bourgeoisie and the proletariat therefore will be resolved in the socialist revolution.

This socialist revolution, the creation of the dictatorship of the proletariat and the construction of a socialist Denmark will create the preconditions for the *final* annihilation of the influence of bourgeois ideology.

What Is KAK?

Kommunistisk Arbejdskrets (KAK)

This is an article from the only English edition of Kommunistisk Orientering *ever published. It appeared on April 10, 1975, as* Communist Orientation *no. 1 and contained a selection of translated essays from* Kommunistisk Orientering *nos. 1-3, 1974-1975. The original Danish version of this article appeared as "Hvad er KAK?" in no. 1 on December 16, 1974. In the English article, English abbreviations were used. These have been changed to the Danish abbreviations in accordance with the usage of abbreviations in this book. Formatting has also been adjusted.*

Kommunistisk Arbejdskreds [Communist Working Circle], KAK, was formed in 1963, when a small group of people either were excluded from the Danish Communist Party, DKP, or left it because they concurred in the criticism of Soviet domestic and foreign policy by the Communist Party of China, and thereby in the criticism of "modern revisionism" as represented at home by DKP.

Some years passed with internal discussions as to the purpose, tasks and social basis of such an "anti-revisionist" organization. As a result of these discussions and through practical work in support of Vietnam and the Palestinian struggle against Zionism, the "theory of the parasite state" gradually crystallized. On the basis of this theory, the *Kommunistisk Ungdomsforbund* [Communist Youth League], KUF, was formed in 1968. As result of renewed discussions on the importance of the theory for the work at hand, KUF merged with the present KAK.

KAK's originally warm and close relations with the Communist Party of China were severed in 1969, because KAK insisted on pursuing a discussion on the connection between Liu Shaoqi's political line and the Comintern's line as it has been familiar in Europe,[1] and because KAK publicly proclaimed its profound disagreement with the Chinese evaluation of what they termed "an unprecedentedly gigantic revolutionary mass movement" amongst the workers of Western Europe and North America.

From 1963 to 1969 KAK published *Kommunistisk Orientering*. The most politically significant articles from this publication have since then been published by Futura Publishing House in booklet form under the titles *There Will Come A Day...* and *Class Struggle and Revolutionary Situation*. KAK's main political and working line is further presented in Gotfred Appel's *The Devious Roads of the Revolution* (1972) and in his preface to [the Danish edition of] V. I. Lenin's *On Imperialism and Opportunism* (1973).

It is KAK's view that the working class in the developed countries of Western Europe and North America occupies a two-fold position. It is at one and the same time exploited (in so far as it produces surplus value) and bribed (in so far as its standard of living and hence its economic—and cultural—needs and its "trade union" demands are based on decades of sharing in the imperialist world's former colonial, now "neo-colonial" plunder). Furthermore, the bribery factor is today the dominant factor of the two.

This bribery should not be understood in such a way that one can actually calculate how large a part of the wage-packet's contents is payment for the value of labour, and how large a part is bribery. It should be understood as meaning that the whole of the imperialist world's economic, industrial, technical, cultural and social development in the last analysis is based upon robbery and plunder in the former colonies and dependent countries, now the "Third World".

It follows from this that it cannot, in KAK's view, be a task for revolutionaries today to inspire or to take the lead in the economic or trade union

---

1. Liu Shaoqi was one of the CPC's senior leaders in the 1950s and '60s. KAK accused him of sharing the Comintern's position that denied the existence of class struggle under socialism, thereby opposing the views of Mao Zedong. Although Liu Shaoqi was removed from his posts during the Cultural Revolution, Appel demanded a continued discussion. See also Gotfred Appel, *Mao, Komintern og Liu Shao-chi: "Leninismen" ifrågasatt i öst och väst* [Mao, the Comintern, and Liu Shaoqi: "Leninism" Challenged in East and West] (Stockholm: Rabén & Sjögren, 1971). —Ed.

struggle of the working class. Such a struggle in the present situation has not, and cannot have the remotest connection with a struggle for Socialism.

On this front it must be considered a far more correct task to inform the working-class (today one large labour aristocracy) that a new economic development which puts an end to the parasitism and plunder of the Western Hemisphere, ought to be welcomed and, if possible, helped along. At the same time, one must understand quite clearly that it is only this very new economic development—whatever form it might take—that can convince the working-class of this fact. A parasitic, embourgeoisified labour aristocracy cannot be transformed into a revolutionary proletariat through speeches and articles. It still has to undergo a "hard castigation through crises", to use Engels' expression, before it can contribute anything of value.

It also follows from this, that although KAK as early as in 1963 proclaimed as its goal the creation of a revolutionary Communist Party in Denmark, we are not "party-forming" in the sense of the word which is common elsewhere on the Left.

KAK could of course have changed its name long ago to that of "party"— the ideological-political unity of the organization has long made this possible. However, we consider it at best meaningless to undertake such a change of name, since in our view the creation of a revolutionary party must be inextricably linked with an objective social necessity if it is to have any value. In our view, there must be a movement, a considerable movement, in society as a whole and especially in a large section of the working-class before a revolutionary party becomes a necessity and thereby has the possibility of playing an important part in the development of society.

When the economic situation, and with it the political situation, has changed to such a degree that the bourgeoisie begins to force the working-class to revolutionary struggle, a struggle for power in society, a struggle to determine the form of society, then the time will be ripe. Then the working-class will need a well-organised, close-knit vanguard. People who beforehand have mastered Marxist theory will be able to play an important role when a spontaneous movement breaks out amongst the workers and when they "succeed in gaining control over it"—to quote Engels once again. "To gain control over" means in this connection to prove capable of putting forward the correct slogans, of providing the correct leadership. Only those who gain this "control" will at that time constitute the vanguard of the working-class, and they will therefore be the party. The name of the organization is of no avail.

Through this short account of KAK's fundamental view, the tasks at hand have in reality already been formulated. They consist in giving political and practical support to people and to organisations which in one way or another are already fighting the plunder by the Western hemisphere and which thereby are helping to undermine the foundations of the parasite state. They consist in building an organization with political-ideological unity, through this work and through continued investigation and studies of the course of development of the whole world, and with as high a degree of discipline and self-sacrifice as is possible at all times—an organization which will gradually become better and better equipped to discover and determine the turn of events "that will lead the masses to the real, decisive and final revolutionary struggle" (Lenin),[2] and which—when the day comes—can place itself at the head of this struggle and lead it to victory.

---

2. This is a quote from Lenin's text *"Left-wing" Communism: An Infantile Disorder* (1920). —Ed.

Manifest–Communist Working Group: A Short Introduction

M-KA

This introductory text to Manifest–Kommunistisk Arbejdsgruppe, M-KA, was published as a pamphlet in 1986 in Danish, Swedish, and English.

Manifest–Communist Working Group of Denmark is working to obtain a socialist world, first and foremost by supporting liberation movements and other socialist forces in the Third World.

It may, on the face of it, appear strange that a political organization in Denmark focus on solidarity work towards the Third World. Why do we not concentrate our efforts on political work in our own part of the world? This choice of priorities is the outcome of certain fundamental political considerations.

The present world order

Let us take a brief look at what characterizes the present world order. The capitalist system still dominates the world economically, politically and militarily. Capitalist countries produce two thirds of the world's commodities and totally dominate the world market. They also have the strongest military apparatus at their disposal. The socialist countries are still the weakest party—although their military and economic strength is increasing. Indeed, the imperialist system is not so much threatened by the socialist/planned economy states as by conflicts within the capitalist system itself.

The capitalist world system is in point of fact characterized by a sharp division into wealthy developed countries (North America, Western Europe, Japan, Australia, New Zealand) and poor underdeveloped countries—the Third World. Centuries of plunder and exploitation of human and natural resources in Asia, Africa and Latin America have led to affluence and development in the imperialist countries, and corresponding misery and underdevelopment in the exploited countries. This division of the capitalist world into imperialist and exploited countries has been—and still is—a necessary precondition for the development of the system; but at the same time, this division also gives rise to social conflicts which threaten to disintegrate the system.

The Third World is the focal point

A retrospective view of developments during the past 30–40 years will show that it is first and foremost areas in the Third World that have constituted the focal point in the struggle against imperialism for socialism.

The Communists' victory in China, the struggle against Dutch colonialism in Asia, the Korean War, the Vietnam War and the other conflicts in South East Asia, the Algerian liberation struggle, the struggle against Portuguese colonialism in Angola, Mozambique and Guinea Bissau, the liberation of Zimbabwe from the settler regime, the liberation struggle in Namibia and South Africa, the numerous wars and conflicts around the settler state of Israel, the victorious struggle for Cuba and Nicaragua, the struggle in El Salvador, Guatemala and Chile—are mere examples from a long series of events which have brought the people's struggle in the Third World into focus.

It is no accident that the Third World is the focal point for the struggle against imperialism. The exploitation of the Third World's population and resources constitutes the very foundation of the existing capitalist world order. The dynamism of the imperialist system brings about a constant tapping of the life blood of the Third World. By virtue of unequal exchange, values to the tune of hundreds of billions of U.S. dollars are transferred annually. The result of this exploitation is a life in misery and poverty for the population of the Third World, the likes of which is unknown in the imperialist countries.

These circumstances have led to a demand for change on the part of the exploited masses. A demand which the imperialist countries and their local allies seek to suppress with all the means in their power. This is the main cause of the constant unrest in the Third World.

On the other hand, the exploitation and underdevelopment of Asia, Africa and Latin America has been a precondition for the rapid development of capitalism in USA, Canada, Western Europe, Japan, Australia and New Zealand. It has likewise been an essential precondition for the economic progress and social security which by and large the whole working class in the imperialist countries has won for itself. It is this division of the capitalist system into poor and wealthy countries which is a prerequisite for the development of the system, which forms the background for the so-called North-South Conflict.

The anti-imperialist forces

The Communist Movement, more or less regardless of which part of the movement one cares to consider, has traditionally divided the anti-imperialist forces into three categories:

a. The socialist countries,
b. The working class and other progressive elements in the developed capitalist countries,
c. National liberation movements and other socialist forces in the Third World.

Let us consider what role these various categories play in today's anti-imperialist struggle.

a) The socialist countries

It is hardly accidental that the "socialist countries" are always mentioned first in publications issued in these countries. The fact of the matter is that these countries consider themselves to be the leading force in the anti-imperialist struggle. The correctness of this assertion is, however, very much open to question. As mentioned earlier, a concrete examination of the past 40 years' anti-imperialist struggle will show that it has mainly been the liberation movements and the socialist forces of the Third World that have been the spearhead in the confrontation with imperialism. Nor is it such that these movements are a product of, or have been exported from the Soviet Union or the other socialist countries, as the USA is especially fond of claiming. There may well be grounds for arguing that, for example, the revolution in Nicaragua has sought inspiration and experience from Cuba or other socialist countries and movements, but the origin, development and success of the Sandinist revolution is first and foremost a result of circumstances in Nicaragua itself.

It is correct that the Soviet Union especially has often played an important role for the success of revolutionary movements. The military balance of power between East and West, which the Soviet Union has succeeded in achieving in the course of the 1970s, has limited USA's possibilities for unrestrained aggression in the Third World, and has increased the socialist countries' ability to provide struggling movements and newly established progressive states with material and political support, thereby increasing their chances of victory and survival.

It is also true that the Soviet Union has increased its global influence through this involvement in the Third World, *but* the reason that the Soviet Union has been able to play this role lies beyond Soviet control, insofar as it lies in the economic/political development in the Third World itself.

Because of the imperialist countries' economic and military strength, the socialist countries have been in a permanently difficult position. Right from the establishment of the first socialist state in 1917, the developed capitalist countries have exerted enormous economic, military and political pressure on the planned economy states, partly in the hope that they might collapse, partly to prevent them from providing support to the anti-imperialist struggle in other parts of the world. In order to survive, the socialist countries have consequently been forced to give top priority to their own defense. The primary concern of the Soviet Union and the other socialist countries has always been the defense and development of "existing socialism". They have supported the anti-imperialist struggle in the Third World to the extent that this did not conflict with their own short term security interests, which means first and foremost—as long as this did not have the effect of provoking the imperialist counties. The liberation movements and socialist forces in the Third World, on the other hand, give highest priority to direct confrontation with imperialism and its local flunkeys, which is only natural. They have nothing to lose.

The fact that the socialist countries and progressive movements in the Third World face a common enemy and have the same goals makes them potential allies. They both have the *strategic* goal of conquering imperialism and replacing capitalist exploitation with a socialist world order. For the Third World, this is a necessary prerequisite for a solution of the enormous social problems with which they are faced—and the socialist countries cannot feel secure, and their economic development will be hampered, as long as imperialism exists. But the developed socialist states and the movements of the Third World often adopt differing tactical positions in their confrontations with imperialism.

One might speak of a tactically offensive and a tactically defensive position. The liberation movements and the socialistically oriented movements in the Third World are in the frontline, in a strategic and tactical offensive. They have everything to win and nothing to lose. The socialist countries, on the other hand, occupy a tactically defensive position. As long as the imperialist system retains its present strength, they must constantly defend their dearly won independence. There is thus nothing directly treacherous in this defensive policy, though on occasions it might appear somewhat opportunist.

MPLA, FRELIMO or Nicaragua's Sandinists were offensive, uncompromising movements as long as they were fighting for state power. Today, having achieved state power, they have to use a considerable part of their resources to defend themselves against enemies within and from outside. Such as the relative distribution of power is in the world of today countries such as Nicaragua, Angola or Mozambique cannot support revolutionary movements in neighboring countries without encountering considerable problems. They have to carefully assess the relative distribution of power regionally and internationally, together with the nature and extent of their support in order not to jeopardize their own revolution. Revolutionaries must therefore rely first and foremost on their own strength.

b) The working class in the developed capitalist countries

In keeping with the traditional categorization, the second part of the anti-imperialist front is said to constitute the working class in the imperialist countries. Let us take a closer look at the role that this class has actually played in the anti-colonial and anti-imperialist struggle.

The spreading of capitalism over the whole world at the end of the last [19th] century led partly to the creation of one integral economic system—one world market, but partly also to a division of the capitalist system into an exploited and an exploiting part. In the previous century, the living conditions of the proletariat in Europe and in the colonies were by and large equally miserable. From around the turn of the century, however, this state of things began to change. The working class in the imperialist countries succeeded, slowly but surely, in securing increased wages and an extension of their political rights. During the first half of the 19th century, the capitalist system had been unable to meet, let alone fulfill the proletariat's demands for better living conditions. This was beyond what the capitalist system could provide at this point in history. But this state of affairs changed decisively with the onset of imperialism. Colonial profits made it possible for the ruling class to meet the demands of the working class without jeopardizing the existence of the system itself. Rising wages, improved working conditions and the extension of political rights served also to strengthen working-class belief in the possibilities of reformism, which in turn made it possible for the bourgeoisie to extend political rights and so forth. The rising wage level –financed through imperialism's exploitation of Asia, Africa and Latin America– led moreover to a steadily growing domestic market in the imperialist countries and thus to a dynamic development, which in turn resulted in stable social and political conditions.

The development of the welfare states in the imperialist countries resulted in a change in the nature of the contradiction between the working class and the bourgeoisie. A class struggle does, of course, still exist. Regardless of whether wages are high or low, the social product under capitalism consists of two inversely proportional parts, namely the wages of the working class and the profit of the capitalists. An increase in one of these elements results in a corresponding decrease in the other. Therefore the contradiction still exists. But when the national exploitation to which the working class is subjected constantly diminishes when compared with the advantages the class enjoys by belonging to a rich privileged nation, then there comes a point when the increase in the national affluence becomes more important than the struggle against capital. It is not only the bourgeoisie, but also the working class in the imperialist countries that benefits from the low wages in the Third World and the resultant low prices of the products from these countries. Cheap raw materials from the Third World for industry and agriculture in the imperialist countries lead to cheap finished products when measured in relation to the relatively high wages in the wealthy countries. If wages in the Third World were raised to a Western European level, then products such as copper, tin, chromium, zinc, coffee, tea, cocoa etc. would become several hundred percent more expensive. Also cheap finished products such as textiles and electronics are produced in the Third World. At the same time, the high wage level in the imperialist countries means that commodities from these countries are beyond the means of workers from the Third World with their poor wages.

Thus, imperialism has meant that the working class in the imperialist countries and the proletariat in the exploited countries do not at the present time share the same interests. In practice this has also proved to be the case. One would have great difficulty finding an example of the English working class having supported the anti-colonial struggle that took place within the Empire. By and large, it has supported the changing governments' colonial policies throughout the past 100 years, from Ireland to Southern Africa, from India to the Falkland Islands. Nor indeed can the French working class boast of having supported Vietnam's, Algeria's or Syria's struggle for independence—far from it. Generally speaking, the working class of USA has also rallied around the imperialist and anti-socialist policy of this country throughout the world. When the people of USA nevertheless did eventually turn against the Vietnam War, they did so not in solidarity with the Vietnamese people, but because the war was beginning to cost too many *U.S.-American* lives. Generally speaking, the workers of the Western World are pro-Israeli and consider the Palestinians to be terrorists. The working class of the imperialist world does not favor Apartheid, yet they certainly do not wish to have a socialist South Africa either. Anti-communism has increased in the Western World in recent years. The microscopic Left, which does after all exist in the imperialist countries, has never wished to face these facts, but has instead always excused the working class. "The workers have been indoctrinated by schools, TV, radio and the bourgeois press—they do not know any better." But to explain decades of consistent opportunism as the result of Social Democratic betrayal is to bid farewell to historical materialism. The working class has not been misled, but pursues policies which are consistent with the interests and goals of the working class. To claim that the bourgeoisification of the working class is the result of indoctrination and the propaganda of the mass media is an equally shoddy excuse. Why, one might well ask, is the proletariat of the Third World, which is exposed to reactionary propaganda in at least equal measure, not equally bourgeoisified—and why is the imperialist working class so receptive to bourgeois and anti-socialist propaganda? No—the attitude of the working class in the Western World towards the anti-imperialist struggle is rooted first and foremost in economic facts. The working class does not want a new world order which will involve it having to forfeit privileges. It will be naive of the liberation movements and socialists of the Third World to count on the active support of the working class in the Western World for a radical transformation of the present world order.

c) The liberation movements and the socialist forces of the Third World

It is thus our conviction that the Third World constitutes the most important front in the anti-imperialist struggle. Anti-imperialism is, however, a broad concept. It may cover nationally minded capitalists who wish to protect their own industry and domestic market against foreign competition, or religious fundamentalists who wish to fight "foreign" cultural and religious influence, or yet again petit bourgeois strata in the armed forces and administration who wish to pursue particular national goals. Finally, there are the liberation movements and socialists who, in addition to national and cultural liberation, also fight for economic liberation.

Since World War 2 the countries in the Third World, with a few exceptions, have achieved formal national independence. This process has not, however, injured imperialism in any decisive way or led to any general solution of the economic and social problems facing the Third World. We are of the opinion that only the socialist forces of the Third World will be in a position to undertake an effective continuation of the anti-imperialist struggle.

This struggle must be carried out on two planes: the national and the international. On the national plane, this means a struggle against capitalist exploitation and the constructing of a socialist national order, which by means of a planned economy can ensure an optimal use of human and material resources for an economic and politically democratic development of the country. On the international plane—a struggle for a new economic world order, which can put an end to international exploitation. Poverty in the Third World is closely bound up with these countries' connection with the capitalist world market. Even if e.g. Zaire [today's Democratic Republic of Congo] carried out a socialist revolution tomorrow, the price of their most important source of income, copper, would not rise. Neither does Nicaragua get more for its coffee or bananas because it has had a socialist upheaval. Regardless of the economic policy which has been in force in the now independent countries, they have had to learn through experience of how their individual efforts to develop their economies have been hampered by the conditions that prevail on the world market. The struggle against the present economic world order is therefore a very important element in the liberation of the Third World. Only through a national revolution combined with international solidarity between the countries of the Third World will it be possible to back up the demand for a new economic world order with sufficient force. It is first and foremost the socialists in the Third World who are the guarantors for this political strategy.

We believe that a progressive development in the Third World have to be a socialist development. We support the forces, who after gaining national liberation want to continue the revolution towards economic and social liberation. We find material support work most important—sympathy and moral support is not sufficient.

In short, this is our political line.

What Can Communists in the Imperialist Countries Do?

M-KA

This is a chapter from the book Unequal Exchange and the Prospects of Socialism, *authored by M-KA and published in English by their press Manifest in 1986. The Danish version of the book, titled* Imperialismen idag: Det ulige bytte og mulighederne för socialisme i en delt verden *[Imperialism Today: Unequal Exchange and the Possibilities for Socialism in a Divided World] was published by Manifest in 1983. The chapter's original title is "Hvad kan kommunister i de imperialistiske lande gøre?"*

As inhabitants of one of the richest countries in the world, our possibilities of promoting socialism are limited because of very special conditions. In the richest imperialist countries there are no classes today which are objectively interested in overthrowing the imperialist system, because all classes in these countries profit by this system. Any social movement in the rich imperialist countries must be seen in the light of this fact. A mass movement has only a socialist perspective if it is directed against imperialism. Such a mass movement does not exist in the imperialist countries.

For decades left-wing parties in Western Europe and North America have set themselves the task of leading the struggle of the working class for higher wages, improved conditions, etc. This practice has been followed irrespective of the special position of the working class in the imperialist countries. Therefore they are reformists, no matter what international ideals they have had, whether they were pro-Soviet, -Chinese, or -Albanian, and regardless of their names. It cannot be the task of the Communists to lead the struggle of the labour aristocracy and thus to maintain or increase its privileges.

Support the Anti-Imperialist Movements
in the Exploited Countries!

As anti-imperialist mass movements are only found where imperialism means exploitation and impoverishment, the task of the Communists is to support the movements there. The most effectual practice of Communists in an imperialist country today is to support the anti-imperialist liberation movements in the Third World who fight against capitalism and international exploitation and for socialism. By supporting movements who pursue an anti-imperialist policy and who have the necessary political strength because of a mass basis, or who have the possibilities of developing such a strength, we can do our share towards impairing imperialism.

We support the national revolutionary movements in the underdeveloped countries because these social movements represent the biggest possible social improvement in their countries; because, through a revolution, they have the possibilities of liberating enormous productive forces, especially in the form of human labour power; because, through the efforts of establishing a socialist society in their own country, they take a step towards the establishment of socialism in the whole world, also if these countries are not in a situation in which they can establish a socialist society immediately. There is no direct or easy way from an underdeveloped and exploited economy to socialism. In spite of this, the national movements in these countries represent the greatest threat to the imperialist system today. They do their share towards creating crises in imperialism. These crises are of crucial importance, if a revolutionary situation ever is to arise in the rich part of the world.

Unlike the capital and the labour aristocracy, the Communists are interested in crises in capitalism. Therefore, when the crises arise, it is not the task of the Communists to defend the privileged position of the labour aristocracy by making plans to protect the capitalist system against crises. Communists in the imperialist countries should not try to reduce the extent of such crises and their consequences such as unemployment, decreases in wages, etc. Even today, when the economic crisis has meant only a comparatively small decrease in the standard of living of the population in the rich countries, the "fear of crisis" is widespread. The left-wing parties, from the Social Democratic party to the extreme left wing, compete with the right-wing parties to suggest the most efficient methods of solving the problems of capitalism. To them it is first and foremost a question of defending the standard of living achieved. The revolutionary perspective of the crisis has been completely forgotten. From a revolutionary point of view, crises are necessary. When the crisis is really felt, the Communists must oppose chauvinism, racism and hatred towards immigrant workers, and support anti-imperialist movements and progressive states in the Third World.

In the long view, the crises can only be removed by an elimination of capitalism through a global revolutionary socialist development. It is however evident that only the economic development itself can convince the labour aristocracy of this. The labour aristocracy, which helps to administer imperialism, cannot be transformed into a revolutionary class exclusively by means of agitation and propaganda. It is primarily the economic development that determines the policy of a class.

Support the Liberation Movements Materially!

The way in which Communists of imperialist countries can support the liberation movements is of course specific from country to country. However, one thing is sure: if the support is to be of any importance, it must primarily be of a material nature. At the end of the 1960s, members of our organization participated in and tried to influence the big demonstrations directed against the warfare of the United States in Vietnam. But even though much was written about it and there were many discussions, and even though thousands of people were engaged in the work even in a small country like Denmark, the material support to the Vietnamese liberation movement was surprisingly small.

During this period the left wing devoted quite some time to liberation movements all over the world, but there was a striking disproportion between the often very militant and uncompromising slogans and the minimal value it had to the liberation movements and their struggle. The majority of the left wing did not concern themselves with the liberation movements with the primary aim of supporting them, but rather because they hoped to mobilize more people. People whom they could engage in their work for the labour aristocracy in Denmark with the illusory purpose of leading its wage struggle in a socialist direction. In the 1970s this became even more obvious. It was not possible to transfer the few anti-imperialist forces from the Vietnam work to the support of the liberation struggle in the Southern Africa, Palestine, etc. Other questions have caught the main interest of the left wing. Anti-EEC[1] and anti-nuclear power campaigns, pollution problems, environmental questions, unemployment problems etc. Anti-imperialism is no longer an important aspect of the political activity of the left wing. It is a very limited number of people that can be mobilized for anti-imperialist work in Denmark today.

However, it is positive that here and there in the imperialist countries there are supporting groups which attach the greatest importance to material support. By this work, the possibilities of the liberation movements for defeating imperialism are improved. Talks with representatives of the liberation movements and visits to the movements have confirmed that it is of use to offer material support, as they often lack the most elementary things to be able to carry on their struggle and to be able to mitigate the hardships of the masses.

What Do We Work For?

It is our aim to gather anti-imperialists in order to support the struggle against the suppression and exploitation of the Third World. As things are now it must be a matter of individuals, as there is no objective basis for mass movements with anti-imperialist views in Denmark today.

The solidarity for which we work is not based on pity or bourgeois humanitarianism, but on the awareness that the emancipation of the proletariat in the exploited countries is a condition of the destruction of the imperialist system and the introduction of socialism in Denmark.

We regard the two aspects of the political struggle, theory and practice, as inseparable. It is necessary continuously to investigate the economic and political conditions in the world in our endeavours to increase and improve our support, and to find new ways in which we can give this support. We have to study which contradictions are the most important, so that our efforts are

---

1. EEC stands for "European Economic Community," a predecessor to the European Union. —Ed.

concentrated on the areas which will be of most benefit to the struggle for socialism. We shall communicate our views to the anti-imperialist movements and states in the Third World and to anti-imperialist groups and organizations in all countries. In particular, we shall discuss our opinion of imperialism and the economic and political conditions in Western Europe. For a long time the left wing has passed on its illusions about the conditions in Europe and the solidarity of the working class with the liberation movements. We shall continue to tell the liberation movements not to count on an active support of their struggle on the part of the labour aristocracy. On the contrary, they must expect opposition, and this is not due to ignorance or lack of information about the struggle, but to the position of the working class of the imperialist countries as a labour aristocracy—a global upper class.

The starving and exploited masses shall be victorious!

APPENDIX

Acronyms of Political Organizations

ANC (African National Congress): founded in 1912, the ANC played a decisive role in the South African antiapartheid struggle under the leadership of Nelson Mandela; today, it is South Africa's ruling party.

BCM (Black Consciousness Movement): a grassroots antiapartheid movement that emerged in the 1960s and focused on the organizational autonomy of blacks and people of color in South Africa; after its most prominent representative, Steve Biko, died in police custody in 1977, the legacy of the BCM was carried on by a variety of different organizations, among them the short-lived communist group Isandlwana Revolutionary Effort, IRE, named after the site of the first major battle in the Anglo-Zulu War of 1879.

CPC (Communist Party of China): founding and ruling party of the People's Republic of China.

DBS (Danmarks Socialistiske Befrielseshær): "Denmark's Socialist Liberation Army" was a clandestine group that claimed responsibility for a number of arson attacks on corporate targets around Århus in the early 1980s.

DFLP (Democratic Front for the Liberation of Palestine): see PFLP.

DKP (Danmarks Kommunistiske Parti): the Communist Party of Denmark, founded in 1919, reached its height after World War II with many of its members credited for their active resistance against the Nazi occupation; allied with the Soviet Union during the Cold War, the DKP was represented in the Danish parliament until the 1970s; today, it is a part of the Red-Green Alliance (Enhedslisten–De Rød-Grønne).

FARC (Fuerzas Armadas Revolucionarias de Colombia): the Revolutionary Armed Forces of Colombia are a Marxist-Leninist guerrilla organization active since 1964.

FMLN (Frente Farabundo Martí para la Liberación Nacional): the Farabundo Martí National Liberation Front was founded as a coalition of left-wing guerrilla movements in El Salvador in 1980; today, it is a left-leaning political party.

FNL (Front National de Libération): Marxist-Leninist resistance and liberation movement in South Vietnam, active from 1954 to 1976 and commonly known as the Viet Cong (in English also as the National Liberation Front, NLF).

FNLA (Frente Nacional de Libertação de Angola): Angolan national liberation movement founded in 1954; today a center-right political party.

FRELIMO (Frente de Libertação de Moçambique): Mozambique Liberation Front, founded in 1962 and a driving force in Mozambique's independence struggle; embraced Marxism-Leninism from 1977 to 1990 and remains the country's ruling party to this day, now as a member of the Socialist International of Social Democratic parties.

FSLN (Frente Sandinista de Liberación Nacional): socialist liberation movement in Nicaragua, commonly known as Sandinistas, responsible for the overthrow of the authoritarian regime of Anastasio Somoza in 1979; today, the FSLN rules Nicaragua as a Social Democratic party.

IRE (Isandlwana Revolutionary Effort): see BCM.

KAK (Kommunistisk Arbejdskreds): Danish Marxist-Leninist organization founded by Gotfred Appel and others in 1963; the so-called Blekingegade Group emerged from it in the 1970s; dissolved in 1980; published the journal *Kommunistisk Orientering*.

KAP (Kommunistisk Arbejdarparti): see KFML.

KBW (Kommunistischer Bund Westdeutschland): the Communist League of West Germany was a Maoist organization founded in 1973 and dissolved in 1985; it was one of the most influential of the numerous German "K-groups" (K for *kommunistisch*).

KFML (Kommunistisk Forbund Marxister-Leninister): the Communist Alliance of Marxist-Leninists was a Danish Maoist organization founded by former KAK members in 1968; the KFML turned into the Kommunistisk Arbejdarparti [Communist Workers' Party], KAP, in 1976 (dissolved in 1994).

KUF (Kommunistisk Ungdomsforbund): KAK's youth chapter, founded in 1968, dissolved in 1975; published the journal *Ungkommunisten* from 1968 to 1970.

LSM (Liberation Support Movement): North American anti-imperialist organization focusing on support of Third World liberation movements; active from 1969 to 1982.

MAG (Marxistisk Arbejdsgruppe): a short-lived (1978–1980) Marxist organization that formed after the KAK split in 1978.

M-KA (Manifest–Kommunistisk Arbejdsgruppe): emerged as a Marxist organization after the KAK split in 1978; named after its journal *Manifest*, which was published from 1978 to 1982 (later, the name stood for a publishing house); the organization's core group was more or less identical with the Blekingegade Group members.

MPLN (Movimento Popular de Libertação de Angola): the People's Movement for the Liberation of Angola was founded in 1956 on Marxist-Leninist principles, played a decisive role in the Angolan independence struggle, and has ruled Angola since independence in 1975, today belonging to the Socialist International of Social Democratic parties.

PAC (Pan Africanist Congress of Azania): founded in 1959 as a pan-Africanist split from the ANC, PAC was an important force during the antiapartheid struggle; today, it remains a small political party.

PFLO (Popular Front for the Liberation of Oman): the PFLO emerged from the Marxist Popular Front for the Liberation of the Occupied Arabian Gulf (later, Popular Front for the Liberation of Oman and the Arab Gulf), PFLOAG, which was involved in armed resistance against the Sultanate of Oman from the late 1960s into the 1970s; it existed as a political organization until the early 1990s.

PFLOAG (Popular Front for the Liberation of the Occupied Arabian Gulf/ Popular Front for the Liberation of Oman and the Arab Gulf): see PFLO.

PFLP (Popular Front for the Liberation of Palestine): founded in 1967 as a pan-Arab organization pursuing the establishment of an independent Palestinian state, the PFLP soon embraced Marxism-Leninism; the best-known among its breakaway factions are the Syrian-based Popular Front for the Liberation of Palestine–General Command, PFLP-GC, founded in 1968 as an action-oriented organization critical of Marxist ideology, the Democratic Front for the Liberation of Palestine, DFLP, a Maoist organization founded in 1969 (originally as the Popular Democratic Front for the Liberation of Palestine, PDFLP), and the Popular Front for the Liberation of Palestine–Special Operations (also known as External Operations or Special Operations Group), founded by Wadi Haddad in the early 1970s and focusing on high-profile international actions.

PLO (Palestine Liberation Organization): a Palestinian umbrella organization founded in 1964 with the aim of establishing an independent Palestinian state; today, widely recognized as the official international representative of the Palestinian people; after Fatah, founded by Yasser Arafat in 1965, the PFLP is the PLO's second-strongest faction.

RAF (Rote Armee Fraktion): the Red Army Faction was a German urban guerrilla movement founded on anti-imperialist principles in 1970.

SED (Sozialististische Einheitspartei Deutschlands): the Socialist Unity Party of Germany, founded in 1946 as a merger of the German Social Democratic Party (Sozialdemokratische Partei Deutschlands, SPD) and the German Communist Party (Kommunistische Partei Deutschlands, KPD) in the Soviet occupation zone, was the ruling party of the German Democratic Republic, GDR, commonly known as East Germany.

SWAPO (South West Africa People's Organization): founded in 1960, SWAPO was the driving force in the Namibian independence struggle and has been the ruling party since Namibia's independence in 1990; it belongs to the Socialist International of Social Democratic parties.

TTA (Tøj til Afrika): "Clothes for Africa" was a Third World solidarity project founded by KAK in 1972; dissolved in 1986 and replaced by Café Liberation, which closed in 1989.

UNITA (União Nacional para a Independência Total de Angola): the National Union for the Total Independence of Angola was founded in 1966 and was, besides the MPLA, the main force during the struggle for Angola's independence; engaged in a twenty-seven-year-long military conflict with the MPLA after independence in 1975, it is today a center-right political party and the country's second-largest.

ZANU (Zimbabwe African National Union): formed in 1963 and the driving force in the Zimbabwean independence struggle; Zimbabwe's ruling party since independence in 1980 (today, officially named Zimbabwe African National Union–Patriotic Front).

Timeline

1963

» KAK, the journal *Orientering* (from October 1964, *Kommunistisk Orientering*), and the publishing house Futura founded

1964

» Gotfred Appel travels to China for the first time to meet with CPC representatives

1966

» KAK founds the Vietnamkomité

1968

» KUF, the journal *Ungkommunisten* and the Anti-imperialistisk Aktionskomité founded; Peter Døllner, Holger Jensen, and Jan Weimann are among the first KUF members

1969

» KAK's collaboration with the CPC ends

1970

» Niels Jørgensen joins KUF

» Gotfred Appel and Ulla Hauton visit PFLP representatives in Jordan

» KUF members are involved in riots during protests against the World Bank summit in Copenhagen

» *Ungkommunisten* ceases publication

1971

» Torkil Lauesen joins KUF

1972

» Tøj til Afrika (TTA) founded

1973

» January 10: burglary at a Danish Army weapons depot in Jægerborg, Copenhagen

1975

» December 9: robbery of
a cash-in-transit truck
on Nordre Fasanvej in
Copenhagen (500,000 crowns)

1976

» September 2: robbery at the
Lyrskovgade post office in
Copenhagen (550,000 crowns)

» November 8: postal money
transfer scam in Copenhagen
(1.4 million crowns)

1977

» KAK's "anti–gender
discrimination campaign"
begins

1978

» KAK splits into three different
organizations: KAK with
Gotfred Appel and Ulla
Hauton (dissolves 1980), MAG
(dissolves 1980), and M-KA
with Peter Døllner, Holger
Jensen, Niels Jørgensen,
Torkil Lauesen, and Jan
Weimann (dissolves 1989
after the Blekingegade Group
members' arrest)

1980

» September 15: Holger Jensen
dies in a traffic accident

1982

» Karsten Møller Hansen and Bo
Weimann join M-KA's illegal
activities

» work on the Z-file begins

» April 2: robbery of a post office
at Vesterport, Copenhagen
(768,000 crowns)

» November 9: burglary at a
Swedish Army weapons depot
in Flen

1983

» March 2: robbery of a cash-
in-transit truck in Lyngby (8.3
million crowns)

1985

» Rausing kidnapping plans
abandoned

» Peter Døllner leaves M-KA

» September 27: Blekingegade
apartment rented

» December 3: robbery at
the Herlev post office in
Copenhagen (1.5 million
crowns)

1986

» Tøj til Afrika turns into Café
Liberation (opens in April
1997)

» December 22: robbery at
the Daells shopping center
in central Copenhagen (5.5
million crowns)

1988

» Bo Weimann leaves M-KA

» November 3: Købmagergade
robbery (13 million crowns)

1989

» April 13: Peter Døllner, Niels
Jørgensen, Torkil Lauesen, and
Jan Weimann arrested

» May 2: Carsten Nielsen injured
and arrested following a
car accident, Blekingegade
apartment discovered, Karsten
Møller Hansen arrested

» August 10: Bo Weimann
arrested

1990

» September 3: trial against the
Blekingegade Group members
begins

1991

» May 2: the Blekingegade
Group members are sentenced
to prison terms ranging from
one year (Peter Døllner) to ten
years (Niels Jørgensen, Torkil
Lauesen, and Jan Weimann);

» October 14: Marc Rudin
arrested in Turkey

1993

» April 28: Marc Rudin
extradited to Denmark

» October 20: Rudin sentenced
to eight years in prison

1994

» April 2: Carsten Nielsen
released from prison

» April 8: Bo Weimann released
from prison

1995

» December 13: Niels Jørgensen, Torkil Lauesen, and Jan Weimann released from prison

1997

» February 18: Marc Rudin deported to Switzerland

2007

» Peter Øvig Knudsen's two-volume history of the Blekingegade Group, *Blekingegadebanden*, is released

2009

» the documentary film *Blekingegadebanden* and the TV series *Blekingegade* are aired

» the article "Det handler om politik" ("It Is All About Politics"), authored by Niels Jørgensen, Torkil Lauesen, and Jan Weimann, appears in *Social Kritik* no. 117, March 2009

Convicted Blekingegade Group Members

The years in parentheses relate to KUF, KAK, or M-KA membership, not necessarily involvement in the illegal practice.

> Peter Døllner (1968–1985), sentenced to 1 year
> Niels Jørgensen (1970–1989), sentenced to 10 years
> Torkil Lauesen (1971–1989), sentenced to 10 years
> Karsten Møller Hansen (1978–1987), sentenced to 3 years
> Carsten Nielsen (1987–1989), sentenced to 8 years
> Bo Weimann (1978–1988), sentenced to 7 years
> Jan Weimann (1968–1989), sentenced to 10 years

Currency Conversion

Approximate exchange rates between the U.S. dollar and the Danish crown:

> January 1972, 1 = 7.1
> January 1975, 1 = 5.7
> January 1978, 1 = 5.8
> January 1981, 1 = 6.0
> January 1984, 1 = 9.9
> January 1987, 1 = 7.4
> January 1990, 1 = 6.6

Literature

For literature by and about KAK, M-KA, and the Blekingegade Group please consult the excellent website www.snylterstaten.dk, which also contains most of the (limited) material available in English. A notable publication is the 1994 book *Blekingegade 2, 1th*, written by Betina Bendix and Lene Løvschall, which is the only Danish book that contains interviews with the former Blekingegade Group members Niels Jørgensen, Torkil Lauesen, Carsten Nielsen, and Jan Weimann.

ABOUT PM PRESS

PM Press was founded at the end of 2007 by a
small collection of folks with decades of publishing, media, and organizing experience. PM Press
co-conspirators have published and distributed
hundreds of books, pamphlets, CDs, and DVDs.

Members of PM have founded enduring book fairs,
spearheaded victorious tenant organizing campaigns, and worked
closely with bookstores, academic conferences, and even rock bands
to deliver political and challenging ideas to all walks of life. We're old
enough to know what we're doing and young enough to know what's
at stake.

PM Press is always on the lookout for talented and skilled volunteers,
artists, activists, and writers to work with. If you have a great idea for
a project or can contribute in some way, please get in touch.

PM Press
P.O. Box 23912
Oakland, CA 94623

www.pmpress.org

FRIENDS OF PM PRESS

These are indisputably momentous times—the financial system is melting down globally and the Empire is stumbling. Now more than ever there is a vital need for radical ideas. Friends of PM allows you to directly help impact, amplify, and revitalize the discourse and actions of radical writers, filmmakers, and artists. It provides us with a stable foundation from which we can build upon our early successes and provides a much-needed subsidy for the materials that can't necessarily pay their own way. You can help make that happen—and receive every new title automatically delivered to your door once a month—by joining as a Friend of PM Press. And, we'll throw in a free T shirt when you sign up.

Here are your options:

- **$30 a month** Get all books and pamphlets plus 50% discount on all webstore purchases
- **$40 a month** Get all PM Press releases (including CDs and DVDs) plus 50% discount on all webstore purchases
- **$100 a month** Superstar—Everything plus PM merchandise, free downloads, and 50% discount on all webstore purchases

For those who can't afford $30 or more a month, we're introducing **Sustainer Rates** at $15, $10, and $5. Sustainers get a free PM Press T-shirt and a 50% discount on all purchases from our website.

Your Visa or Mastercard will be billed once a month, until you tell us to stop. Or until our efforts succeed in bringing the revolution around. Or the financial meltdown of Capital makes plastic redundant. Whichever comes first.

Fire and Flames:
A History of the
German Autonomist Movement

by Geronimo

Introduction by George Katsiaficas

Afterword by Gabriel Kuhn

ISBN: 978-1-60486-097-9

208 pages • paperback • $19.95

The first comprehensive study of the German autonomist movement in the 1970s and '80s ever published, from its origins in the antinuclear and squatting movements, to the campaign around Startbahn West, and militant protests against the World Bank and IMF. The politics and experiences, challenges and innovations, of the autonomists are examined in this engaged and important study.

Life Under the Jolly Roger:
Reflections on Golden Age Piracy

by Gabriel Kuhn

ISBN: 978-1-60486-052-8

272 pages • paperback • $20.00

Tracing the history of pirates, with attention paid to dynamics around race, gender, sexuality, and disability in the communities establsished by these nomadic outlaws, along with their forms of organization, economy, and ethics. Illuminated by insights from a wide range of thijnkers, from Marshall Sahlins and Pierre Clastres to Mao Zedong and Eric J. Hobsbawm via Friedrich Nietzsche and Michel Foucault.

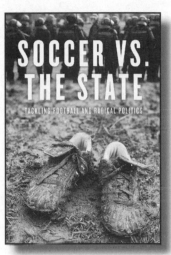

Soccer vs. the State: Tackling Football and Radical Politics

by Gabriel Kuhn

ISBN: 978-1-60486-053-5

264 pages • paperback • $20.00

From its roots in working-class England to political protests by players and fans, and a current radical soccer underground, the notion of football as the "people's game" has been kept alive by numerous individuals, teams, and communities. This book not only traces this history, but also reflects on common criticisms that soccer ferments nationalism, serves right-wing powers, and fosters competitiveness. An orientation for the politically conscious football supporter and an inspiration for those who try to pursue the love of the game away from television sets and big stadiums, bringing it to back alleys and muddy pastures.

Sober Living for the Revolution: Hardcore Punk, Straight Edge, and Radical Politics

edited by Gabriel Kuhn

ISBN: 978-1-60486-051-1

304 pages • paperback • $22.95

Straight edge has persisted as a drug-free, hardcore punk subculture for 25 years, with an ambiguous political legacy – associated with self-righteous macho posturing and conservative puritanism, but also with radical thought and activism. Sober Living for the Revolution *explores this complex history.*

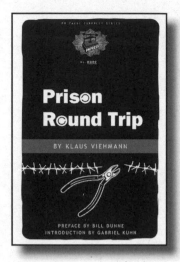

Prison Round Trip

by Klaus Viehmann

Preface by Bill Dunne

Introduction by Gabriel Kuhn

ISBN: 978-1-60486-082-5

28 pages • pamphlet • $4.95

First published in German in 2003, the essay's author had been released from prison ten years earlier, after completing a 15-year sentence for his involvement in urban guerilla activities in Germany in the 1970s. It is a reflection on prison life and on how to keep one's sanity and political integrity within the hostile and oppressive prison environment; "survival strategies" are its central theme.

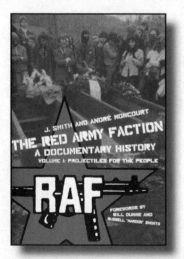

The Red Army Faction
A Documentary History
Volume 1: Projectiles for the People

by André Moncourt and J. Smith

Forewords by U.S. political prisoners
Bill Dunne and Russell "Maroon" Shoats

ISBN: 978-1-60486-029-0

736 pages • paperback • $34.95

For the first time ever in English: all of the manifestos and communiqués issued by the RAF between 1970 and 1977. From Andreas Baader's prison break, through the 1972 May Offensive and the 1975 hostage-taking in Stockholm, to the desperate, and tragic, events of the "German Autumn" of 1977. Separate thematic sections address the context from which the RAF emerged and within which it managed to repeatedly renew its base of support and carry out its daring anti-imperialist attacks.

Settlers: The Mythology of the White Proletariat from Mayflower to Modern

by J. Sakai

ISBN: 978-1-62963-037-3

456 pages • paperback • $20.00

J. Sakai shows how the United States is a country built on the theft of Indigenous lands and Afrikan labor, on the robbery of the northern third of Mexico, the colonization of Puerto Rico, and the expropriation of the Asian working class, with each of these crimes being accompanied by violence. In fact, America's white citizenry have never supported themselves but have always resorted to exploitation and theft, culminating in acts of genocide to maintain their culture and way of life. This movement classic lays it all out, taking us through this painful but important history.

The Red Army Faction
A Documentary History
Volume 2: Dancing with Imperialism

by André Moncourt and J. Smith

Introduction by Ward Churchill

ISBN: 978-1-60486-030-6

480 pages • paperback • $26.95

This work addresses a period in which the RAF regrouped and reoriented itself, with its previous 1970s focus on freeing its prisoners replaced by a new anti-NATO line. Includes details of the RAF's operations, and its communiqués and texts, from 1978 up until its 1984 offensive. Changes in both the guerilla and the radical left are addressed during what was a period of resurgent protest and political violence in West Germany.

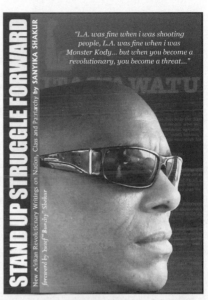

KER SPL EBE DEB

Since 1998 Kersplebedeb has been an important source of radical literature and agit prop materials.

The project has a non-exclusive focus on anti-patriarchal and anti-imperialist politics, framed within an anticapitalist perspective. A special priority is given to writings regarding armed struggle in the metropole and the continuing struggles of political prisoners and prisoners of war.

The Kersplebedeb website provides downloadable activist artwork, as well as historical and contemporary writings by revolutionary thinkers from the anarchist and communist traditions.

Kersplebedeb can be contacted at:

Kersplebedeb
CP 63560
CCCP Van Horne
Montreal, Quebec
Canada
H3W 3H8

email: info@kersplebedeb.com
web: www.kersplebedeb.com
       www.leftwingbooks.net

Kersplebedeb